sex secrets
of the
kama
sutra

& other *Eastern pleasures*

sex secrets
of the
kama
sutra

& other *Eastern pleasures*

Kayla Ricci

LONDON, NEW YORK, MUNICH,
MELBOURNE, DELHI

Project Editor Suhel Ahmed
Project Designers Emma Forge, Tom Forge
Senior Art Editor Nicola Rodway
US Editor Shannon Beatty
Production Editor Maria Elia
Senior Production Controller Man Fai Lau
Creative Technical Support Sonia Charbonnier
Photography John Davis
Art Direction for Photography Emma Forge
Managing Editor Penny Warren
Managing Art Editor Glenda Fisher
Art Director Lisa Lanzarini
Publisher Peggy Vance

First American edition, 2011

Published in the United States by
DK Publishing, 375 Hudson Street, New York, NY 10014

11 12 13 14 15 10 9 8 7 6 5 4 3 2 1
001—179000—Sept/2011

Copyright © 2011 Dorling Kindersley Limited
All rights reserved

Published in Great Britain by Dorling Kindersley Limited.

A catalog record for this book is available from the Library of Congress

ISBN: 978-0-7566-7557-8

DK books are available at special discounts when purchased in
bulk for sales promotions, premiums, fund-raising, or educational use.
For details, contact: DK Publishing Special Markets, 375 Hudson Street,
New York, New York 10014 or SpecialSales@dk.com.

Printed and bound by Tien Wah Press, Singapore

Discover more at **www.dk.com**

DK encourages safe and responsible sex
- Use condoms to reduce the risk of contracting or transmitting sexually transmitted diseases (STDs).
- Ensure that you and your new partner have been tested for STDs before engaging in any unprotected sexual activity.
- Speak to your doctor if you have any concerns about your sexual health.

Contents

Introduction
An erotic venture **into the East**

Imagine retiring to a gorgeously prepared bedchamber with your lover and abandoning yourselves to nights of erotic pleasure. Picture yourselves teasing and delighting each other with an inspiring selection of techniques and positions that you have never tried before. By taking you on a sumptuous journey through the East, *Sex Secrets of the Kama Sutra* will teach you both to become gloriously talented lovers along the way.

The first stop on your erotic journey is India. Chapter one reveals the secret techniques of the *Kama Sutra* and the *Ananga Ranga*. You can try out everything from methods of "mouth congress" and thrusting techniques, to classic *Kama Sutra* positions such as Twining and Fixing a Nail. You will also discover how to have ecstatic sex, Tantric-style.

Chapter two reveals the heady delights of Arabian sex. Make your lover swoon using arousing fragrances, frolics, and foods, then drive his or her passion wild with novel sex positions.

China is the next stop on your sexual voyage. Immerse yourselves into the ancient erotic secrets of *The Tao*. You will discover that a slow and prolonged approach to sex can give you intense waves of joy and make orgasm a whole-body experience. Following on, Chapter four lifts the lid on the Japanese art of eroticism. By entering the secret world

of *Geisha*, *Shunga*, and *Shibari*, you can explore sex that is sensual and kinky. If you have ever fantasized about tying up your lover, or experimenting with erotic domination and submission, you will find techniques here that are safe yet extremely sexy.

Within each chapter the sex positions are arranged in order of erotic intensity, starting with sensual (for when you want a loving mood) and moving up to steamy, raunchy, passionate, and, ultimately, ravishing, for when you want to express your wanton lust. Each position also has an "expert rating" to let you know how easy or challenging it is (one "brush stroke" is the least challenging while five equals the most challenging). The pages are also sprinkled with quotes from ancient erotic manuscripts, and from real-life contemporary lovers who were candid enough to share their experiences. Let yourself be inspired by the quotes and the "secrets," as well as by the gorgeous photography. Finally, so that you can relax fully into the erotic pleasures, make sure that sex is always safe, legal, and mutually pleasurable—and remember that if you are using oil it can damage the latex in condoms, rendering them ineffective. In techniques where the use of oil is mentioned and you are using condoms, the oil should be replaced with a water-based lubricant.

spicy pleasures
from
India

"Desire is the heart's way of reaching into the unknown ..." *KAMA SUTRA*

Spicy pleasures from India
the world of the *Kama Sutra*

The *Kama Sutra* is the oldest Hindu guide to the art of erotic love, written between 1 and 4 BCE. The book's most charming aspect is its open approach to the heady and sensual delights of sex. Its author, Vatsyayana, compares sexual pleasure to food, and describes sex as a means of sustaining the body and nourishing a relationship.

Although widely believed to be a manual of sex positions, the *Kama Sutra* is actually much more. It is a guidebook for the entire erotic lives of both men and women, dispensing advice for almost every romantic or sexual issue they might encounter.

All-embracing Vatsyayana starts by describing the perfect environment for lovemaking, offering sugggestions on how to create it (see p13). And, once you are inside this love chamber and feeling amorous, he tells you exactly how to embrace each other to ensure peak arousal before having sex (see pp18–19). He even addresses sensitive issues such as genital compatibility, explaining how to make sex work when you and your lover are mismatched in terms of size and "fit" (see pp42–43).

For him and her Vatsyayana dispenses specific advice to men and to women. Men, for example, are instructed on grooming and personal hygiene, how to be successful with women, how to recognize signs of sexual interest, how to seduce a virgin, and how best to thrust during intercourse (see pp44–45).

Vatsyayana gives equally detailed advice to women. He instructs virgins on how to flirt with a man, and courtesans on how to give a man what he desires. Wives are schooled in how to keep a husband happy (including fashion and home maintenance tips). In addition, women are briefed on when—and how—to take on a dominant role in the bedroom (see p34).

Sexy and sensual Although modern lovers may choose not to embrace all of Vatsyayana's teachings about love and relationships, many of the sexual recommendations are not only timeless, but also hot and sexy. There is very little that is taboo in the *Kama Sutra*, and it is fascinating to discover that the sex acts practiced in ancient India—for example, oral sex, anal sex, threesomes, spanking, and biting —were considered as kinky as they are today.

Another aspect of the *Kama Sutra* that is relevant to us today is Vatsyayana's suggestion that we should immerse ourselves in sensual pursuits. He believed that lovers should be able to find pleasure both in and out of bed. He recommended that lovers learn sensual skills, such as massage, mixing perfumes, preparing wines and juices, reading poetry, and playing musical instruments … all significant for a night of seduction and pleasure.

"When he entices her, he does it gently, for **women are like flowers**, and need to be enticed with tenderness. He uses an embrace that she likes. When he has placed **his hand on her thighs** and succeeded in caressing them, he moves his hand upward in stages." *KAMA SUTRA*

in the temple **of love**

Sexy spaces
making a **love chamber**

Lovers in the time of the *Kama Sutra* considered sex to be an erotic ceremony, something to be cherished and lovingly prepared for. Making a love chamber—a room perfect in every detail for the act of love—was an important part of the preparation. The intention was for lovers to be enveloped in a mood of tranquil eroticism the moment they stepped inside.

In the past The ancient Indian love chamber would have looked gorgeous. It may have had whitewashed walls, fans, plump pillows, a bed draped in satin sheets, a beautifully shaped musical instrument, such as a lute, hanging from a peg, and garlands of flowers … plus anything the lovers might need during the night, such as lemon bark to fragrance the mouth or oils to rub into the skin.

Set the scene You do not have to redecorate your bedroom to make it into a love chamber. One of the simplest things you can do is remove clutter: take away anything that doesn't look, smell, or feel gorgeous, or doesn't inspire sensuality (such as computers, phones, clocks, bills, work files, or dirty laundry).

Try dressing the bed in clean, fragrant, and soft fabrics—sheets you want to lie naked on. Put flowers by the bed, or place a single rose on the pillow. Or as one ancient Indian love manual cheekily suggests, leave a book on display—one that contains "amorous songs and gladdens the glance with illustrations of love postures."

Create the mood Replace lamps and harsh lighting with tall candles, so that you can enjoy the experience of making love in flickering candlelight, while watching the erotic shadow play of your bodies on the walls. Have a music player in the room and quietly play your favorite sexy music to build up the romantic ambience. Even if it is not practical to keep your room in this minimal state, try it once in a while. Make it part of an anniversary or birthday gift—send your lover an invitation that reads "Come to the bedroom at 8pm." Relish the ceremonial feel of your surroundings.

Beginning congress

preparing your body **for passion**

The *Kama Sutra* advises lovers to pay meticulous attention to personal hygiene. It recommends that one should bathe every day, rub limbs with oil every other day, shave the face (men) every fourth day, and remove body hair every tenth day. In doing so, couples enhance the lovemaking experience because their bodies are more appreciated by each other.

Sweet anticipation Today's lovers get ready for sex for the same reasons as the lovers in Vatsyayana's era did: they enjoy the ritual of erotic preparation, they want to feel and look gorgeous, and they want to tempt and entice their partner.

Smooth, fragrant skin Step into a hot bubble bath and, before you start to wash, close your eyes and savor the feeling of being immersed in the hot water. Now make your skin smooth by exfoliating it with a sweet-smelling body scrub or polish. Alternatively, rub shower gel into your skin with a loofah or an exfoliating glove. Pay attention to every surface and crevice, from your toes (which should be sweet and suckable) to your neck (which should be smooth and kissable).

Step out of the bath and pat yourself dry with a soft towel. Then rub oil or moisturizer into your skin. This will leave your skin smooth, and incredibly receptive to a lover's touch. Finally, spray yourself with a fragrance that you both adore. For an added touch of romance, try preparing for passion with your lover. Invite your partner into the bath and wash him or her all over using slow, caressing strokes.

Sensual thoughts Preparing your body gives you a chance to enter the mood. As you go through the ritual of preparation, your thoughts will automatically turn to sex. The more you abandon yourself to these thoughts, the more aroused you will be when you finally slip between the sheets. So, while you wash yourself, imagine your lover's hands caressing you. And as you spray scent on yourself, picture your lover up close to your skin, inhaling the gorgeous scent.

Secret

grooming the hidden place

The *Kama Sutra* advises the grooming of pubic hair. Nowadays many men and women appreciate the erotic benefits of keeping that area well tended. Leaving just a token strip or triangle (or any other shape) of pubic hair looks and feels sexy, plus being suitably trimmed can intensify sexual sensation and can also make oral sex more enjoyable for both partners.

Women can take this a step further. Once you have a bare and silky pubic triangle, make it look stunning with stick-on crystals or jewels designed specifically for this purpose. Now lie in bed wearing just your panties—fix him with a wicked look and invite him to unwrap you like a gift!

"He colors his lips with a ball of moist red lac and fixes it with a small ball of beeswax. He puts a ball of sweet-smelling mouthwash in his cheek and takes some betel in his hand to use later." *KAMA SUTRA*

Side-by-side Clasping

This highly intimate position lets you build up to sex slowly.
FOR BOTH Start by lying on your sides in bed together, talking and touching. Make your conversation increasingly flirtatious or romantic, with lots of eye contact. Then, as things heat up, touch each other more purposefully. When you are both turned on, you need only move your bodies a little bit closer for him to penetrate.
FOR HIM If he needs help to find his way in, she can move higher up along his torso and rest her upper thigh on his waist.

The beauty of Side-by-side Clasping is that you are both in an equal position, so you can take turns moving and pleasuring each other. Keep gazing at each other, too—it will drive the intensity of your desire to dizzying heights.

It's sensual because ...
you can take your time giving each other gorgeous caresses. Try trailing your fingertips along the side of your lover's body and then lean in for a meltingly soft kiss. Stroke your lover's nipples and genitals at the same time. It's an ideal position to appreciate each other's bodies.

❝We lay on our sides talking while **gazing into each other's eyes**. Then we started touching each other and the mood got really hot until she reached out and **pulled me into her.❞**

Twining

Try this position when you are both highly aroused and in the mood for sex that is incredibly hot and intimate. She lies back on the bed and pulls him into her. Once your bodies are locked together she raises her leg in the air and twines it around his body to hold him in place. **FOR HER** Now she is in a position to reach up and run her fingers through his hair or give tingling caresses to his neck, cheek, or jaw. Or, if she prefers, she can pull him down for an emotionally intense kiss. **FOR HIM** He can enjoy the gentle pressure of her calf pulling him closer inside her and, because his pelvis is pressed firmly against hers, he feels deeply and pleasurably enclosed. You can then work together to find an intoxicating rhythm that rocks you both to a heady orgasm.

It's sensual because …

he takes his weight on his hands so she is free to completely relax her upper body and concentrate on blissful internal sensations as he thrusts. Her hands are also free to stroke him affectionately, and there is lots of eye contact.

Twining of the Creeper
and other **erotic embraces**

One of the secrets of sensational sex is to use foreplay techniques that drive your lust incredibly high. This way, at the moment of penetration, both of you are burning with desire. A very sexy foreplay technique is to twine your bodies around each other in intimate and seductive embraces. The *Kama Sutra* offers a number of embraces, depending on the mood you are in.

Twining of the Creeper To experience the full impact of this standing embrace, do it when you are both naked and can enjoy the closeness of your bodies. She wraps her arms around his waist in a tender embrace, while twining her leg around his thigh in a posture that is said to be like a "vine twisting round a great dammar tree" (see right). She then puts one hand behind his neck, gazes lovingly at him, and bends his face toward hers for a kiss.

The Grinding Embrace Try this explosive move when you are both still dressed, and for a frisson of naughtiness, do it in a public place. Go up to your lover, slide your hands around their waist, and pull their hips toward you. Now press your pelvises tightly together and grind against each other for, as the *Kama Sutra* delicately puts it, "not too brief a time." You need not exchange any words—the action is enough to express your sudden sexual urge to each other.

For a slight variation, press your lover against a wall before making this move. The wall acts as a buttress so you can grind more vigorously. Vatsyayana calls this The Pressing Embrace.

Milk and Water Lovers are advised to try this embrace when they are already naked and highly aroused, since it is an embrace that can easily graduate into a sex position. He sits on a chair or on the edge of a bed as she stands astride him and sits down slowly on his lap. Then she wraps her arms and legs around his body and presses herself to him, crushing her breasts against his chest (see opposite, top). Now "embrace as if you would enter one another," says the *Kama Sutra*, and feel the heat of each other's bodies.

Secret
make her fizz ...

The *Kama Sutra* recommends a move called "Embrace of the Thighs." Men can try this on their lover while standing up (either dressed or naked). Press her against a wall and give her a slow and sensual kiss. As you sense her becoming more aroused, slip your thigh between hers and apply gentle pressure. As her passion mounts, push your thigh more tightly against her while clasping her buttocks and pulling her toward you. Not only will she revel in being dominated, but she will also find the clitoral pressure electrifying.

envelop your **lover**

Rice and Sesame Imagine the difficulty of separating a mixture of rice grains and sesame seeds. This is the intensely close connection that Vatsyayana pictured for moments of peak desire. Try Rice and Sesame when you are "blind with passion". There are no strict rules for this. You simply fall onto the bed together, wrap your arms and legs around each other's bodies, then writhe and roll enjoying the feeling of complete rapture. This embrace also happens to be ideal when you are both in a playful mood and want to fool around before making love.

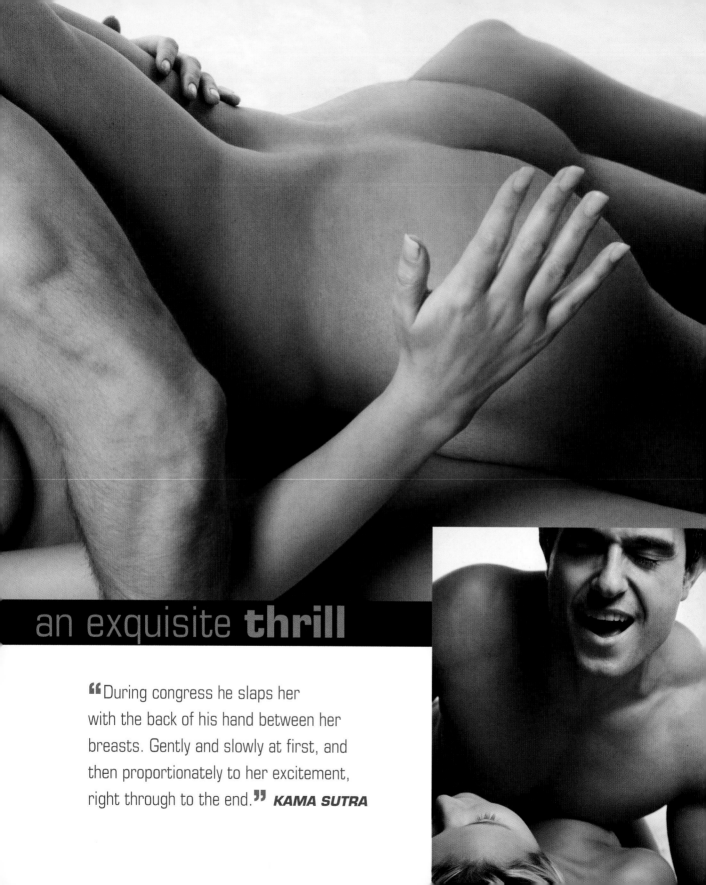

an exquisite thrill

"During congress he slaps her with the back of his hand between her breasts. Gently and slowly at first, and then proportionately to her excitement, right through to the end." *KAMA SUTRA*

Stoking the appetite
striking and spanking (as part of intercourse)

The *Kama Sutra* compares sex to a quarrel that gets more and more heated. "Striking" or spanking each other during sex can make lovers dizzy with pleasure, and drive the quarrel to its natural climax. *Kama Sutra*-style spanking is not about inflicting punishment and pain, but about experimenting with exciting new sensations. Your aim is to make your lover gasp as you send a rush of tingling erotic energy through them. A single well-timed spank during sex wakes up their body and makes it alive to all the "electric" sensations of touch.

Secret

Cobra's Hood

Use this *Kama Sutra* hand position for spanking. Curve your fingers so your hand is in the shape of a cobra's hood—this minimizes pain and maximizes pleasure. Raise your hand and deliver a fast, light spank to your lover's buttock. Then, as they gasp, pull them in toward you for a kiss. If you are the one being spanked, try experimenting with some *Kama Sutra*-style dominance and submission. Shout "no!" or "stop!" while your lover repeatedly spanks you. This kinky technique is designed to drive you both to extreme heights of passion. But do agree on an unrelated "safe" word in case you genuinely do want your lover to stop.

Spanking zones Although the *Kama Sutra* recommends a variety of body parts that can be spanked, the favorite spanking zone for most lovers is the buttock—either the sides, or across the crease so the vibrations ripple pleasurably through the genitals. (Never spank anywhere near the tailbone or the testicles.) Timing is also very important. Right at the beginning of sex you'll both be too intoxicated with the rush of penetration. And, at the height of sex, you will be focused on the build up to orgasm, so a spank can be distracting. Instead, try delivering a spank midway through intercourse. You will discover it has the same erotic effect as a change of sex position: it wakes your body up, stimulates your imagination, and sets off a fresh new wave of arousal.

If you repeat the spank, be sparing. A spank works best as a surprise—a huge part of the pleasure comes from the sudden shock.

Perfect positions If he is doing the spanking, it helps if she is on top of him. Men: try pulling her onto your lap while you sit on an upright chair—this makes it easy to reach the sides of her buttocks. Or ask her to get into an extremely erotic position in which you lie flat on your back and she straddles you with her back to you. Another classic spanking position is for her to bend over in a standing position, while you enter her from behind. Women: if you are doing the spanking, try it during the missionary position (see left) and try to aim for the sides of his buttocks.

Wife of Indra

This incredibly steamy sex position was named in honor of Indrani, the wife of the Hindu god Indra. To get into this position, the woman needs to draw her knees tightly to her chest and raise her buttocks off the floor. The man, kneeling upright, catches her body and pulls her tight against him. The woman nestles her feet against her lover's stomach or chest as he enters her. **FOR HIM** The man moves softly at first and then, as his passion rises, becomes brisker and more vigorous. In this position he is able to penetrate deeply. **FOR HER** Because her vagina is contracted, his penis will fill her completely, leading to more satisfying sensations.

It's steamy because ... her body is bent into a tight, compact shape that makes her feel deliciously exposed and sexy. And he gets the visual stimulation of seeing all the action as he smoothly moves in and out. Communication through eye contact means sensations are magnified for him and her on an emotional level.

"I walk my feet up from his belly to his chest and then **press his nipples with my toes**. That's my sign for him to enter me deeply, and when he does **it always makes me gasp.**"

Fixing a Nail

"This is learned by practice only," says the *Kama Sutra*. The challenge for the woman is to raise her leg and rest her heel on her lover's forehead, and then to hold the position throughout sex.

FOR BOTH The challenge for the man is to make his movements precise and controlled so that her foot can actually stay in place. It is possible to teeter on the brink of orgasm for a long time. And it is ideal for women who enjoy slow, prolonged stimulation.

Ultimately, if you need some more dynamic movements to push you both over the edge, it is easy to slip back into the missionary position. Then he can move freely and she can push her pelvis up to maximize the clitoral friction she receives.

It's steamy because ...

although it might sound restrictive, the precision of movement this position demands makes it a wonderful turn on. You are both mentally in synch. As a result you are able to build up your arousal levels slowly, which makes it possible to teeter on the brink of orgasm for a tantalizingly long time.

Turning Position

This begins as a simple missionary position, but then takes an unusual twist. He pulls out a little way and then gradually rotates his body until he is facing in the opposite direction with his head facing her toes. He keeps the tip of his penis inside his lover throughout the turn, which requires a little bit of practice.

FOR HIM It is a great way to show off male sexual prowess because he needs a strong erection from beginning to end. Unlike the normal in-and-out thrusting movement of intercourse, he receives a different kind of stimulation as he twists. **FOR HER** The woman can enjoy the thrill of watching her lover perform for her. When he has completed the turn, you can both take the chance to ramp up the eroticism: he can kiss and suck her toes while she can rake his buttocks with her fingernails.

It's steamy because ...
the rotating movement of his penis gives her fantastic sensations. She can ask him to pause at the angle she enjoys the most and use the churning motion (see p44). She can also revel in the sight of his sexy bottom, or even dig her nails in to express how turned on she is.

The Top

This is the female version of the Turning Position. This time he lies back on the bed while she slides on top of him. After taking advantage of the face-to-face position with some hot kissing, she sits up and begins her 180° turn.

FOR HER To feel maximum pleasure she can pause halfway through in a side-saddle position and move up and down on his penis. It is also easy for her to slip her hand between her legs in this position for some clitoral stimulation.

When she has twisted all the way and is facing his feet, she can thrill him by leaning back on his chest and moving her hips in slow, tantalizing circles. Or she can lean forward, squat between his legs and bob up and down on him. **FOR HIM** The man's role is to lie back and enjoy watching her perform this maneuver. He can also offer a caressing hand or gently gyrate his hips from below.

It's steamy because ... she is in control of the movement and gets to experience sex from every angle. Meanwhile, he can feast his eyes on the sight of her sexy body, stroke her back, or cup her breasts and tweak her nipples. Moreover, he gets to admire her from all sides.

"The great thing is that she takes the lead in the Top, **guiding me through all the sexy stages**. It's really lots of different positions rolled into one sequence.**"**

In the King's harem
erotic **fantasies**

Fantasies played an important role in the lives of women kept in the royal harem in ancient India. They were forbidden to have sex with any man except the king, but because the king had so many lovers to satisfy, some women, inevitably, ended up feeling frustrated. The *Kama Sutra* records that harem women would sometimes enact fantasies with other women to fulfill their sexual needs.

Sharing your secrets Fantasies are not just for the sexually frustrated. Thrilling fantasies, shared with a lover, are a widely accepted way to add a whole new dimension to sex.

To elicit your lover's secret fantasies, show you are confident enough to share one of your own fantasies first. Take your lover to bed for a sexy cuddle then pique his or her interest by saying "I've never told you this before …", then pause for a few teasing moments before describing your fantasy in seductive detail. Give your lover an intimate glimpse of your inner erotic world, then invite him or her to reciprocate by saying: "…now I'd love to hear one of yours."

If your lover is shy, give encouragement by offering possible scenarios: sex outdoors, a threesome, or a kinky act of submission, domination, or exhibitionism. Coax them gently out of their shell.

Be bold and playful If you are feeling mischievous, have this conversation while you are out on a date with your lover, perhaps whispered across a restaurant table. The erotic power of your confession will make you yearn to finish the date in the bedroom.

Bringing fantasies to life Other times, fantasies beg to be enacted. For example, her dream of walking into his hotel room, then slipping her coat off to reveal her naked body. Or his fantasy of being blindfolded and tied to the bed while she flicks her tongue over every inch of his body. The possibilties are endless!

Whether you describe your fantasies to each other or act them out, try dedicating one night of the week to fantasy sex. Lose yourselves in the spirit of fun and titillating adventure.

Secret
have heady harem sex

Imagine that you and your partner are making love in a royal harem: drape your bed with elegant Indian fabrics in shades of ruby, gold, or deep purple. Arrange candles around the bed in beautiful candle holders, and burn frankincense or myrrh resin to create a sensual and heady atmosphere. Do, however, be mindful of the fire hazards.

❝He should let her know his feelings by outward signs and gestures, and should show her pictures and things with double meanings …**❞** *KAMA SUTRA*

the **erotic** mind

Mouth congress
secrets of **oral sex**

Oral sex was an illicit practice in ancient India. Although some women performed fellatio on their lovers, Vatsyayana records that it was mainly practiced on men by eunuchs. While giving a massage, a eunuch would gradually move his caresses to the man's penis. If the man became aroused, the eunuch would then perform oral sex using eight different steps to bring him to orgasm!

Eight steps to orgasm Women can try replicating these eight steps described in the *Kama Sutra*. According to ancient Indian ritual, she should feign reluctance and express her wish to stop after each step. And each time, the man responds by begging her to continue.

Start with a stroke called the "the casual": take the base of his penis in your hand and slip your lips and tongue lightly up and down over his glans and shaft. Then move on to "biting the sides": bare his glans and "nibble" the sensitive sides with your lips. Follow this with "the outer tongs": press your lips to his glans and suck lightly. (This works best if you do it on his frenulum—the sensitive band on the underside of his penis). Now try "the inner tongs": take the whole of his glans into your mouth with a gentle sucking action, then repeatedly pull away as if you are spitting him out.

Getting hotter The next four phases are designed to make him more excited and, ultimately, to push him over the edge. The next step is "kissing": hold his penis in your hand and kiss it all over. Now move on to "polishing": swap the kisses for licks so that your tongue darts quickly over his shaft and glans, then enclose the whole of his glans firmly in your mouth.

The next step, "sucking the mango," will stimulate him to orgasm: continue holding his penis at the base, but let it penetrate your mouth as far as possible. Now drive your lips and tongue mercilessly up and down with lots of firm, wet friction. Finally, when he is about to climax, swallow up as much of his penis as you can and press your lips firmly against his shaft. This is called "swallowing up."

Secret
slick and wet

Oral sex is the most pleasurable when it is slick and wet, and the build up to orgasm is gradual. This is the reason why the *Kama Sutra* offers the eight-step method. Women should coat his shaft with lots of saliva—this way your lips will glide divinely up and down. If your mouth is not wet enough, suck a candy—this will not only make your mouth wet, but will also make him taste delicious. To give him an extra zing of sensation, choose a menthol flavor. The surprise tingling will add to his feelings of pleasure.

pleasure by mouth

Extra thrill Surprise him by fellating him in a completely different position from usual. Try laying him on the sofa while you kneel on the floor and lean over him at right angles. Or ask him to lie on his side then lie at right angles behind him and push your head through his thighs (so his testicles are nuzzling your chin). For a sense of kinkiness, lie on your back and ask him to get on all fours so his penis is level with your mouth.

Make her fizz The *Kama Sutra's* advice about cunnilingus is that "the way of kissing the yoni, should be known from kissing the mouth". Men can use their erotic imagination to adapt some of the eight steps described. For example, he can start by nibbling and kissing the whole of her clitoral area with his lips, then he can intensify the pleasure by homing in on her clitoral head and sucking it gently. He can then spread her vulva with his fingers in a "V" shape, and zone in on her clitoral head. As she approaches a peak of excitement, he can adapt the "sucking the mango" technique by inserting a finger or two into her vagina and licking her clitoris in fast, rhythmic circles.

❝Some women of the harem, when they are amorous, do the acts of the mouth on the yonis of one another, and some men do the same thing with women. The way of doing this should be known from kissing the mouth.❞ *KAMA SUTRA*

Splitting of a Bamboo

This is a movement rather than a position. The woman first stretches one leg over the shoulder of her lover's body, then lowers it and raises the other leg onto his other shoulder. And she continues to alternate like this throughout. The man is inside her but remains still.

FOR HER The eroticism of Splitting of a Bamboo comes from the fact that the woman is in control: she is deliberately teasing and titillating her lover (and herself in the process). Picture it as a piece of erotic performance art. If she wears sheer black stockings to draw attention to the elegant shape of her legs, it makes it sexier.

FOR HIM If her up-and-down leg movements do not lead to orgasm, there is a simple solution. When he is at the highest point of arousal, she stops her leg raises, pulls him down and invites him to thrust on top in the classic missionary position.

It's raunchy because …

her movements are done with slow but deliberate erotic intent. Meanwhile, his eyes never leave her face as she tantalizes him with each leg raise—he loves watching her take the lead in pleasuring him.

Pair of Tongs

This is one of the simplest but sexiest positions. He lies on his back while she kneels on top and guides him deeply inside her. The "tongs" in the position name refer to the woman's vaginal muscles. **FOR HIM** According to the *Kama Sutra*, the woman must draw the man's penis into her vagina, press it, and hold it there for a long time so that he feels enclosed.

As well as sitting still and squeezing him with her muscles (read about how to do this on page 138), she can massage the length of his penis by bobbing up and down. **FOR HER** She can grind her pelvis back and forth, or in circles to build up intense friction on her clitoris. Many women love this position because it makes it easier to have an orgasm—even if she does not climax through her movements, she can simply caress herself by hand.

It's raunchy because ... she feels powerful and sexy, and he feels excited by the fact that he is being "taken" possession of. She can enjoy a powerful orgasm and he can bask in the thrill of being massaged by her.

❝Pair of Tongs brings out the **naughty exhibitionist** in me. I love thrusting my chest out and writhing on top of him. **I'm in complete control** and this adds to the thrill.**❞**

Half-Pressed Position

He kneels in a dominant and sexy upright position as she lies on the bed before him.

FOR HIM While gazing into her eyes, he then pulls her close and penetrates her as she rests the sole of one foot on his chest and stretches her other leg out behind his body (or on the bed, if it is easier). This position is one step away from the Pressed Position (see p40).

FOR HER The sensations produced by the Half-Pressed Position are slightly less intense than those of the Pressed Position, but with the advantage that there is space between her legs, he can reach down and stroke her clitoris to give extra stimulation.

It's raunchy because ... her foot on his chest forces him to keep his distance, creating a sexy hint of tension. It also means she has ultimate control: if she wants to be on top, she can use her foot to push him back onto the bed. Then she can get up and straddle him.

❝It feels wonderfully sexy to lean over and **watch her writhe**. Sometimes I like to lift her foot up to my mouth and **suck her toes**. This gets her moaning.**❞**

The Swing

This is the perfect position for sex that is incredibly hot. The woman sits with her back to the man and rocks back and forth by bending her elbows up and down, simultaneously sliding up and down his penis as her bottom swings. **FOR HIM** Men love this position because he can gaze adoringly at the curves of her buttocks and be thrilled by the sight of her sliding up and down on his penis. When she moves in fast, light bounces, he is likely to reach a quick peak of excitement. If he needs to slow her down he can put his hands on her hips or buttocks and slow things down. **FOR HER** A sexy way to relax after the Swing is for her to sit back on his lap while he envelops her in his arms.

It's raunchy because ...

what you lose in eye contact and face-to-face intimacy, you gain in eroticism and a sense of naughtiness. Moreover, women can enjoy the unusual angle of entry, plus the vicarious thrill of hearing his moans of pleasure.

Role reversal

when a woman **acts the part of a man**

In ancient India, a virtuous woman was so devoted to her husband that she would treat him as a divine being. Sexually, he was dominant and she would defer to his every erotic need. Yet there were times, the *Kama Sutra* admits, when it was acceptable for the woman to "lay him down upon his back and give him assistance by acting his part."

Loving relief According to Vatsyayana, if a woman noticed her husband getting exhausted during sex, she could, with his permission, come to his aid by getting him to lie down so she could climb on top of him. Then she was free to "act like a man" and "return the actions that he did to her." It was also acceptable for a woman to take charge if she wanted to try something novel, or if her husband was curious about swapping roles.

Set the rules If you have never played domination and submission games during sex before, try this experiment. Women: tell him that tonight you are taking charge. You are not just going to seduce him, you will also choose exactly how, when, and in what position you are going to have sex. You will help yourself to his body and do whatever you feel like doing. The only rule is that he must submit to your whims completely. If he tries to take control, you will pull away and stop whatever you are doing. You can even teasingly threaten to tie him to the bed if he breaks the rule.

Take charge As you begin your evening of seduction, follow your erotic desires. For example, you could explore his body with your lips and tongue, then you could crawl up his body on all fours and demand oral sex. You could use the tip of his penis to stroke your clitoris as you kneel astride him. You could lie beside him and stroke his penis while kissing him passionately. You could jump on top of him and ride him feverishly. You could use your favorite sex toy on him—or tell him to use it on you. Do whatever brings you pleasure. Above all, drop your inhibitions and have fun together.

Secret

the deep squat stroke

The *Kama Sutra* recommends the Pair of Tongs position (see p31) for a woman who is acting the part of a man. This is because she can use her vagina to draw the penis in, "press it, and keep it thus in her for a long time." For an extra frisson of excitement, try this variation: instead of sitting as you straddle him, squat astride him. Once he is inside you, contract your vaginal muscles as hard as you can. Now hold the contraction and bob up-and-down on his penis. Start slow, and get faster until he is moaning with ecstasy. You can rest your hands on his chest for balance, but tweak his nipples now and then to remind him who is in charge.

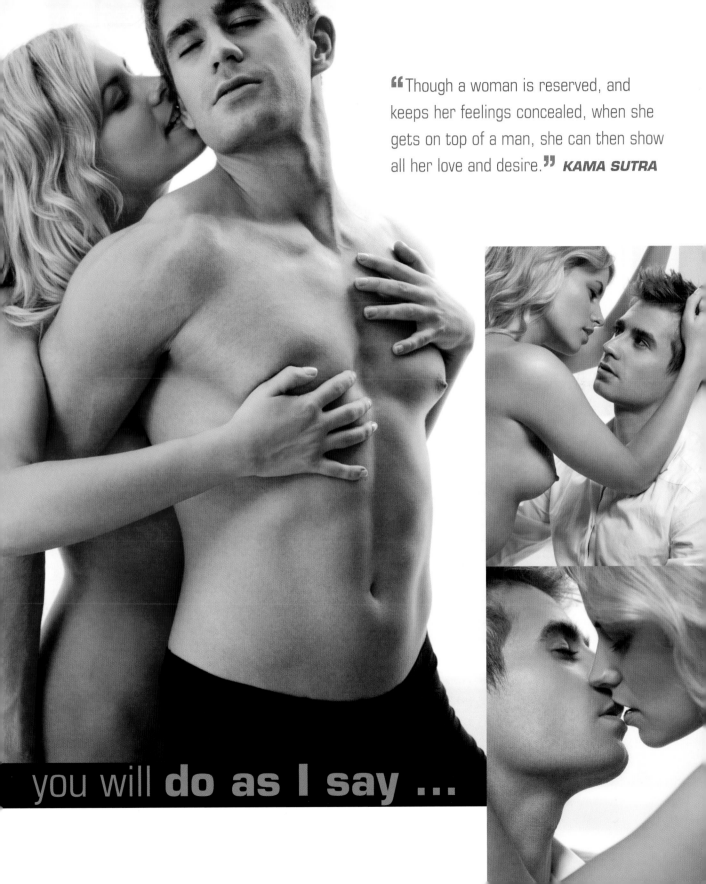

"Though a woman is reserved, and keeps her feelings concealed, when she gets on top of a man, she can then show all her love and desire." **KAMA SUTRA**

you will **do as I say ...**

"Some would say that a woman emits like a man ..."

KAMA SUTRA

Female emission
exploring **the G-spot**

Female ejaculation, far from being a modern discovery, was a hot topic in ancient India. In fact, the *Kama Sutra* debates whether women "emit" in the same way as men. Vatsyayana tentatively suggests that women do ejaculate, but it is rarely seen as women take longer to arrive at this point of emission, which explains why they desire long-lasting sex.

Secret
muscle power

All the Indian erotic texts advise women to exercise their vaginal muscles; and it is now known that strong muscles play an important part in helping women to ejaculate. The more fit and toned her muscles are, the more likely she is to ejaculate when she receives the right kind of stimulation.

Women: try inserting a finger into your vagina and pulling up your muscles to peak contraction. If you can only feel a weak pressure on your finger, start working on your muscles straight away (see p138). Regular muscle workouts will lead to all sorts of benefits to your love life, not just an increased chance of ejaculation.

Take your time Modern science has revealed that some women definitely do ejaculate. It happens when they receive prolonged stimulation to their G-spot. To achieve this, the man is advised to dedicate the evening to her pleasure by exploring the front wall of her vagina (the site of her G-spot) with his fingertips.

Focus on her She needs to be relaxed, so give her a massage with lots of kisses and cuddles. Once she is fully aroused, slide one or two fingers gently inside her and stroke the front wall of her vagina (push your fingertips in the direction of her stomach). Feel for a raised area that is roughly oval in shape and then slowly caress it. (The more aroused she is the easier it is to find her G-spot.) Search for a stroking technique that elicits a gasp or an intense moan— it might be static pressure from your fingertips, a circular rubbing movement, or an in-and-out movement that nudges her G-spot on each thrust. When you discover what drives her crazy, keep doing it.

Double her bliss Intensify her pleasure even more by stimulating her clitoris at the same time as her G-spot. Use the thumb of the same hand that you are using on her G-spot. Or use one hand on her clitoris and the other on her G-spot. If it is difficult, ask her to hold a vibrator against her clitoris, or to masturbate.

Given all this focused stimulation, she will probably reach orgasm quicker than usual. If she is able to ejaculate, she will need to relax her vaginal muscles and push down or let go at the crucial moment (as if she's going to pee). If she doesn't ejaculate, she will almost certainly have an orgasm that will be wonderfully intense.

Elephant

Elephant is the flipped-over version of the missionary position. Instead of lying on her front and parting her legs to invite him in, she does the same lying on her belly. **FOR HER** This creates very different sensations than missionary-position sex because the tip of his penis is angled so that it pushes directly against her G-spot. With repeated pressure or rubbing on the G-spot, some women experience euphoric waves of pleasure. Eventually, making love in this position can lead to an ecstatic G-spot orgasm.

FOR HIM The Elephant position is favored by many men because he can enter her deeply and feel tightly enclosed. And, if he is hitting her G-spot, he can relish the sounds of her gasps and moans. If she's unfamiliar with G-spot sensations, he can experiment to find the depth, angle, and pressure that makes her delirious with pleasure.

It's passionate because ...

he is free to express all his animal lust while she closes her eyes and concentrates on the amazing sensations building up inside her. In addition, there is a lot of skin-to-skin contact throughout, which maintains a deep level of intimacy.

Yawning

She lies back, raises her legs in the air and parts them in a wide V-shape. **FOR HIM** Men love this position because it appears brazen and dramatic—the position of her legs is like an irresistible sexual invitation. As he enters her, he can lean forward and hold her hands for support, or grab her ankles and push her legs farther apart. The Yawning position is for moments of extreme arousal when you both want no-holds-barred sex.

FOR HER Yawning position also works with him in a standing position and her lying on a surface such as a table or a high bed (if she isn't high enough, push some pillows underneath her). This gives him greater freedom to thrust so that she can feel his fullness and fervor completely. But if she wants to slow him down, she can rein him in by crossing her feet behind his back.

It's passionate because ... he finds the position of her body irresistible and plunges in deep. And, as he thrusts, the tip of his penis stimulates some of the highest hotspots in her vagina, making the position intensely pleasurable for both. Every so often he can slow down, lean forward and they can share a kiss.

❝We often choose this position in the build-up to orgasm because it works for us both. **By holding hands we feel intimately connected**, and there's always a lot of eye contact as well.**❞**

Pressed Position

In this position, her legs are bent and clasped by her lover against his chest. Many men and women find the natural dominance and submission of this position incredibly arousing. He towers over her with his legs spread, while she lies curled and compact on the bed. **FOR BOTH** The most erotic movement he can make in the Pressed Position is lightning-fast hip flicks. Her feet push against his chest, which provide him with the means to move his hips sharply, keeping every other part of his body still. The darting strokes of his penis—particularly as the tip moves in and out of her vaginal entrance—can lead to a strong and fast climax for both. If you are in a particularly playful mood and want to raise the eroticism, he can take things even further by tying her ankles together.

It's passionate because ... she feels erotically vulnerable and he feels potent and powerful. If you trust each other, this can produce some intense emotions and lead to a truly memorable sexual experience.

"He loves to **ramp up the tension** when we have sex in the Pressed Position. He presses all the way into me and then pauses. He only starts thrusting when **the anticipation is unbearable**."

Supported Congress

This position is ideal if you are roughly the same height as each other because all he needs to do is crouch slightly to penetrate. It means you can literally have sex at a moment's notice, with no need for a bed or other convenient piece of furniture to lie down on. (This is liberating if you enjoy having discreet sex outdoors, for instance.) **FOR HER** To achieve a deeper penetration, she can lift a thigh and wrap it around his leg, drawing him closer to her. If he is much taller, she can compensate by standing on a step, or he can bend his knees. **FOR HIM** At any point he may choose to assert his dominance and enjoy the thrill of taking the lead. All he has to do is slide his hands under her bottom and lift her up into Suspended Congress (see p47).

It's passionate because ... this is the natural follow-on from a sizzling hot kiss when you are both in a standing position. Maybe you weren't even planning to have sex, but somehow your hands start wandering and you find your pelvises are pressed tightly against each other. Before you know it, you are so turned on that you just begin tearing off each other's clothes!

The stallion and the deer
enhancing your **sexual fit**

The *Kama Sutra* says that sexual fit (having compatible genital sizes) is one of the keys to sexual satisfaction. Vatsyayana describes men as stallions, bulls, or hares—in descending order of penis size. Women, meanwhile, are described as elephants, mares, or deers, depending on vaginal depth. According to the *Kama Sutra*, good genital compatibility leads to the "highest union."

The perfect fit The best sexual unions, in Vatsyayana's opinion, are between men and women with genital sizes that complement one another: a stallion and an elephant, a bull and a mare, or a hare and a deer. And the least satisfying couplings are between a well-endowed man and a tiny woman (a stallion and a deer) or a man with a small penis and a woman with a large vagina (a hare and an elephant). Fortunately, if you do not happen to be the perfect fit, the *Kama Sutra* suggests some enhancement techniques.

Stallions and deers There are many positions that accommodate his penis length so that you both enjoy maximum pleasure. Try any position in which his penis has to reach further than usual, such as Side-by-side Clasping (see p16), or a position in which he stays still and she makes the moves, such as Splitting of a Bamboo (see p30). Most woman-on-top positions (see opposite) are also great for deer women because she is in control. She can hover on the tip of his penis and then descend to the depth she wants to. If you both love penetration from behind, but it makes her feel stretched, she can lie on her stomach with her legs slightly parted. He enters slowly, but his movement is controlled by how far she chooses to open her legs.

Fitting foreplay Most sex positions are possible between a stallion and a deer, but you may need to start slowly with lots of foreplay in which she gets extremely wet and aroused. Men: give your lover oral sex, or take her to near climax with your fingers just before you make love. Women: massage his penis with lots of lubricant before sex—it will help him to slip smoothly inside you.

Secret
extreme arousal

This is a sexy secret for men: if you want to catch her at her tightest, penetrate her when she is at a near-orgasmic level of arousal (or even just after she has climaxed from oral or manual sex).

This works well for a very simple reason: when she is reaching a peak of excitement, she experiences a rush of blood to her genitals. As a result, the lower part of the vagina becomes so engorged with blood that it constricts and naturally hugs the penis tighter than normal.

She will also experience some very enjoyable sensations from the friction created by such a snug fit. It will prolong her state of bliss and may even lead to multiple orgasms.

find the **perfect fit**

Hares and elephants When he is small and she is big, you will get most erotic pleasure from positions that contract her vagina. One of the best positions is for her to lie back and raise her knees to her chest, or for him to take hold of her ankles and push them high in the air (see right).

The key is to explore the angles that create most friction or pressure. Any position that pushes his penis firmly against the front or back wall of her vagina can feel amazing. Women: try sitting on him in Pair of Tongs (see p31) and then leaning back as far as you can. Or bend over and touch your toes as he enters you from behind. Keeping your legs together can create a tighter fit too, especially if you lie flat on your back and he lies on top with his legs outside yours.

Fit and toned vaginal muscles can also make him feel more "hugged" during sex. Read about how to hold him tight from the inside on page 120.

Thrusting secrets
pleasuring her from the inside

Although the *Kama Sutra* is famous for its exotic sex positions, the ancient text also places great emphasis on how to maximize sexual pleasure and provides detailed descriptions of ways to move once you are in a position. Vatsyayana offers men a whole range of thrusting techniques, including Churning and Blow of the Boar to please their lover.

Traditional thrust Most men use the rhythmic, in-and-out thrusts during sex to reach orgasm. The *Kama Sutra* calls this Sporting of a Sparrow and recommends it, but suggests that men should also try some of these alternative strokes beforehand:

Churning and Pressing Before penetration, he can try an incredibly erotic stroke called Churning. Men: hold your penis by the base and use the tip to caress your lover's vulva. Move it in circles around her clitoris and then gently dip it into her vaginal opening before returning to her clitoris. This is a great way of making her wet. Enter her from on top, directing your penis upward with your hand, and make her gasp by nudging her G-spot with your glans (see p37).

Another opening move is for him to enter her as deeply as possible and then to stay perfectly still inside her while pressing his pelvis tightly against hers. This is called Pressing and it allows you to fully savor the ecstatic moments after penetration.

Blow of the Boar When he penetrates her, he angles his penis so that the tip rubs the sensitive front wall. Men: when you find an area that makes her gasp, thrust against it. Make tiny, targeted thrusts rather than plunging in deep. Imagine you are using your penis to massage away an area of tension.

Next, repeat the stroke on a different wall: high up on the back wall of her vagina. There is another pleasure spot there—it is elusive because it is so high up, but, even if it is difficult to find, enjoy the thrill of the search. The act of alternating thrusts against two different walls of her vagina is called Blow of the Bull.

Secret
the Blast of Wind

A *Kama Sutra* stroke called the Blast of Wind is noted for being "dramatic" and can, according to Vatsyayana, make her moan out loud. After a minute of in-and-out thrusting while you are on top, make her gasp by suddenly pulling out completely. Hold yourself in a push-up position by supporting your body weight on your arms. Make the sexual tension ultra-taut by waiting a few moments, then with a fast hip movement, plunge back inside her. The excitement of fast penetration after a brief pause will have an exhilarating effect on her. (It is best not to try this when she is in the final build-up to climax and is relying upon regular, rhythmic thrusts to reach orgasm.)

"When the lingam is in the yoni, and moved up and down frequently, and without being taken out, it is called the Sporting of a Sparrow. This takes place at the end of congress." *KAMA SUTRA*

Suspended Congress

Suspended Congress is an incredibly sexy position. Try it when you want an explosive quickie or a sexually charged reunion. He grasps her thighs or buttocks and lifts her up and onto him. **FOR HIM** While he leans back against the wall, she takes control of the movement by planting her feet on the wall and pushing on and off him.

To add an extra thrill to Suspended Congress, try it in a location that feels risqué. For example, the hallway as soon as you walk in the front door, or in the bathroom at a party. Or even against a wall outside—as long as you do not get caught.

FOR HER He can make her feel truly ravished by first pulling her toward him, then fondling her breasts and buttocks and kissing her ravenously. Then, when you are both at a fever pitch of excitement, he lifts her smoothly onto his erection.

It's ravishing because ... you can both feel the full force of each other's desire. She feels swept away and he feels adored. Even if you fall on the floor at the end, you will remember this position for its intense erotic power.

"I picked her up in my arms and **pressed her against the wall.** We kissed crazily, then I carried her into the bedroom and **we fell into bed.**"

Variant Yawning

She lies back with her knees grazing her nipples. He presses down lustfully on top. Variant Yawning is a relatively easy position to get into (as long as she has supple legs and hips). **FOR HER** It offers extremely deep penetration. So deep, in fact, that men should build up their movements slowly, starting with gentle thrusts and progressing to faster and deeper strokes, which she will savor.

FOR BOTH Variant Yawning is a good grand finale position after several other man-on-top positions. Try this sequence: Twining, Half-Pressed, Pressed, and Variant Yawning (see pp17, 32, 40). With each position her legs move a little higher and the sexual intensity goes up another notch until you reach orgasm.

It's ravishing because …
your faces are tantalizingly close, which means you can both see the intensity of each other's desire. And his deep penetrating strokes combined with the tight connection between your bodies, makes you feel that you are being consumed by each other.

Congress of a Crow
the joy of **69**

Congress of a Crow is the name the *Kama Sutra* gives to mutual oral sex, or "69" as it is commonly known. In ancient India, oral sex was seen as a taboo act, not fitting for upstanding gentlemen. Nevertheless, Vatsyayana realized the pleasure of oral sex and coyly wrote that "it is not without its uses" and each person should make a personal decision about whether to indulge.

Oral sex Even though oral sex in the "69" position is no longer taboo, it still feels deliciously naughty. Just the idea of it can inflame the libido. Instead of having penetrative sex, make Congress of a Crow the main sex event of your night. Adopt an ardent approach as though there is nothing in the world you would rather be doing.

Position yourselves The best position is to lie side by side and top to tail. This feels comfortable so that both of you can concentrate on giving and receiving pleasure. No one is dominant, and you don't have to support each other's weight. Arrange yourselves so that your heads are aligned with each other's genitals, and either rest your heads on each other's thighs, or get comfortable with cushions so you can stay in position for as long as you need to.

Start slowly: teasingly lick, nibble, and nuzzle each other's inner thighs. Run your fingertips over each other's backs, sides, and buttocks. Moan softly as desire sweeps through your body. And, as the mood gets hotter, zone in on each other's genitals.

Perfect pacing The key to good "69" is a keeping a matched pace. Although you don't have to reach orgasm at the same time, you do need to be pleasuring each other at similar speeds. If she is feverishly licking him while his moves are slow, the effect isn't the same. Build up in unison to a frenzy of movement and ecstasy. If one of you is lagging behind, slow things down. Use your hands to give top-up stimulation if you need to. She can tickle his testicles or stroke his perineum. He can insert his fingers into her vagina as he swirls his tongue on her clitoris. The result will be mind-blowing.

Secret
follow the leader

Take turns to lead in the 69 position. This way one person at a time gets to set the tempo, mood, and technique. When your lover is leading, do your best to copy whatever moves he or she is making. For example, if she is giving him slow butterfly licks on his penis, he should do exactly the same to her clitoris. If he is sucking her clitoris and gently caressing her vagina with his fingertips, she should suck his glans in the same manner and lightly tickle his testicles. You will quickly discover that this is a great way to get exactly the kind of touch you crave, and you do not even have to put any of your requests into words.

mutual **delight**

"When a man and woman lie down in an inverted order, with the head of the one toward the feet of the other, and carry on mouth congress, it is called 'Congress of a Crow'." **KAMA SUTRA**

Lower congress
erotic anal **techniques**

Anal sex or anal play can yield some amazingly rich sensations of pleasure. The fact that nerve endings are concentrated in the anal area makes it a highly sensitive erogenous zone. The *Kama Sutra* describes anal sex as "sex below" or "lower congress" and mentions that it was practiced during Vasyayana's time by people living in the "southern countries."

Preparation Contrary to popular belief, anal sex does not have to be uncomfortable, rough, or dirty. It can be sensual and intimate, as long as you prepare correctly. Start by giving your lover an anal massage to make him or her receptive and tingling with pleasure.

Erotic massage Undress your lover and ask him or her to lie on their front. Now kneel or sit lightly astride the back of your lover's thighs and drip lots of warm massage oil onto the buttocks. Slowly smooth the oil into the skin with your hands, performing swirling strokes over the cheeks. Then introduce your fingertips to your lover's anus and perineum by smoothing your hands between the buttocks. Keep your anal strokes brief and fleeting at first, then target the anus more directly. Press lightly on the anal entrance and stroke one fingertip around it in slow circles. Vary the pressure to see what your lover enjoys most. Make sure you use lots of oil or lubricant.

A step further If your lover is happy to go further, gently push your lubricated finger into the anal entrance and explore the rectum. Try pushing your finger in and out slowly. Women can push deeper to give him a G-spot massage (see p158). Men can try stroking the front wall of her rectum (in the direction of her belly), as the perineal sponge lies just beyond, which is highly receptive to stimulation. If your lover tenses up, stop until you feel the muscles relax again. If your lover is new to anal play, keep asking him or her how it feels. Make sure your touches are light and sensual; any kind of force will be resisted with clamped muscles. The more relaxed and aroused your lover is, the more open to exploration he or she will be.

Secret
for giving her ultimate pleasure

To intensify her sensations, men can try to stimulate multiple erogenous zones at the same time. Lie side by side and then work your way down with a trail of kisses, starting from the neck to the navel, and then beyond. Caress her clitoris with your tongue while you circle your finger on her anus. Take your time and let yourself be guided by her moans and gasps. Slide a finger into her vagina, too (but always avoid touching her vulva with anything that has touched her anus, as this risks spreading bacteria).

Women can use the same technique to make him convulse with pleasure; give him an anal massage while stroking his testicles and licking his penis.

take it slowly

"The people in the southern countries have also a congress in the anus that is called the 'lower congress'." *KAMA SUTRA*

The world of the *Ananga Ranga*
more spicy pleasures from **India**

Whereas the ***Kama Sutra*** viewed sex as a sensual art to be enjoyed by everyone, the *Ananga Ranga* was written specifically for married couples, and husbands in particular. The result is a fantastically comprehensive manual of sex instructions explaining the subtleties of foreplay and lovemaking to ensure that couples maintain a healthy physical relationship throughout thier marriage.

Become an artful lover The *Ananga Ranga* was written in 15 or 16 BCE by Kalyana Malla, a Brahmin and a courtier. He believed that all men should study the erotic scripts. This, he said, would allow them to become wonderfully appreciative lovers who would know "how delicious an instrument woman is when artfully played upon; how capable she is of producing the most exquisite harmony … and of giving the divinest pleasures."

Meticulous approach Kalyana Malla was a methodical writer who used lists and categories to present his teachings. The *Ananga Ranga* begins by listing the "four orders" of women, then goes on to categorize the four types of female genitals, the eight methods of embracing, the ten techniques for kissing, the seven ways of erotic biting, and so on.

It even suggests that there are four techniques for erotic hair pulling, called *keshagrana*. In the first, the husband holds his wife's hair behind her head while kissing her lower lip. In the second, he pulls his wife toward him by the back of her hair and kisses her. In the third, he seizes the hind knot of her hair while standing up. In the fourth, husband and wife both grasp each other's hair as they make love.

Sex positions Kalyana Malla gives sex positions the same treatment. He offers different categories and sub-categories of a position, always with the aim of introducing novelty so that couples can experience as many physical sensations as possible.

The breadth and range of techniques and positions is an inspiration to modern lovers (in all kinds of relationships—not just married ones). But perhaps the most profound secret is that sexual bliss often lies in the smaller details. For example, in the way she softly moans when he kisses her lips; the way he pushes cushions under her body to create the perfect angle for penetration; or even the way she makes the bed look gorgeous and then sits in the middle of it with that special look of amorous expectation sparkling in her eyes.

Fun in variety By embracing the immense variety of techniques the *Ananga Ranga* offers, you can keep your sex life exciting, fun, and fresh—indefinitely. Or in the words of Kalyana Malla: "I have in this book shown how the husband, by varying the enjoyment of his wife, may live with her as with 32 different women, ever varying the enjoyment of her and rendering satiety impossible."

"This book is composed with the object of **preventing lives and loves being wasted**, and the benefits from its study are set forth ... those men ignorant of the scripture of Cupid must be looked upon as foolish and unintelligent ..." *ANANGA RANGA*

Come hither
secrets of **flirting**

The *Ananga Ranga's* view of flirting between couples has much in common with modern dating advice: lots of eye contact, flattery, laughter, and light touching. Women are encouraged to engage in sexy displays that draw a man's eye to her body. As Kalyana Malla says of the amorous woman: "she delights in walking before us and displaying her legs or her bosom."

Lover's gaze The *Ananga Ranga* recognizes the erotic impact that staring longingly at a lover can have. It says that a woman loves a man when she is not ashamed of fixing her gaze on him "without deference." Lustful looks can be especially smoldering when you fantasize about caressing someone while you are looking into their eyes. Your erotic intent will be obvious from the way you hold your gaze, especially if you raise a brow and pout a little at the same time.

Even if you know your lover inside out, sharing a prolonged gaze with him or her can feel excitingly provocative. Try it when you are out together with a group of people—a few seconds of eye contact across a room can sometimes feel more provocative than several minutes of flirty conversation or even touching.

Seductive flattery Kalyana Malla says that praising and flattering the person you admire is a good way to express sexual interest without being too direct. Try to make your compliments sincere and tailored specifically to the person you are flirting with.

You can also flatter someone in subtle non-verbal ways: try leaning toward the person as he or she speaks. The subtext is that you are so interested in the person that you don't want to miss a word. Or try copying the person's movements: as they pick up their drink, you pick up yours; as they lean forward, you lean forward; as they touch their hair, you touch yours. The person will sense that you are subtly attuned to them, but won't necessarily know why.

Gently teasing someone, making the person laugh, and laughing when he or she says something funny are indirect forms of flattery,

Secret
give a sexy gift

A lot of people suffer a crisis of confidence when it comes to flirting with someone they like. If flirtatious words and gestures are not your style, give your intended lover a gift instead. It is a form of flattery that both men and women love.

The *Ananga Ranga* suggests tasty delicacies, flowers, perfumes, and particularly preparations of sandalwood, musk, and saffron. A gift that evokes one's sense of smell or taste will show them that you are a sensual lover. If you are already in a relationship and wish to stoke the fire of passion again, buying gorgeous underwear, or a book that contains something meaningful, (such as a poem you both love) will be cherished enormously.

when your **eyes meet ...**

which can create a bond. Kalyana Malla tells men that many woman who are flirting with you will respond to a question with "joking and jesting words" instead of giving a straightforward answer.

Erotic exposure For women, the *Ananga Ranga* favors the bold approach of exposing sexy body parts, though this also needs to be sutble and playful. He describes the gestures of an amorous woman teasing her lover: "She draws her dress over her bosom, apparently to readjust it, but leaves her breasts partly exposed."

Try leaning forward to expose your cleavage; hitch up your skirt a little to reveal your thighs; or let your top fall to expose one of your shoulders. Touching the places you want to be touched is another powerful technique: fleetingly touch your lips, neck, or chest with your fingertips. If he is attuned to your intentions, his eyes will follow.

❝She strokes her own cheeks (so as to entice her husband). ... She bites her lower lip, chewing it as it were. At times she looks ashamed without a cause (the result of her own warm fancies).**❞** *ANANGA RANGA*

Crying-out Position

This is sex at its most intimate. She nestles herself on his lap and rests her legs on his forearms. Then both of you can abandon yourselves to a slow and heartfelt kiss. For extra tenderness, try occasionally pulling away and gazing deeply into each other's eyes. **FOR HER** She can lift her chin and tip her head back while he plants featherlight kisses along the side of her neck. Another way for him to show affection is to thread his fingers through her hair so she can rest her head on his palm as they kiss.

FOR BOTH Although movement is a little restricted in this position, you can enjoy the sensuality of being so intimately connected. But if you need more hard and fast stimulation, he can easily lie down on his back so she can get into the Pair of Tongs position (see p31).

It's sensual because ... you feel enclosed inside a bubble, both emotionally and physically. Your hands are free to stroke and caress each other; and the combination of your lips locked in a kiss while his penis is deeply enclosed inside her feels sublime to both partners.

"Without uttering a single word, **he lifted me onto his lap,** slid his arms under my legs, and suddenly he was inside me—**it was incredibly erotic."**

Crab Embrace

If you like warm, cozy sex on a cold winter's night, this is the ideal position. You are literally wrapped up in each other. As well as sharing body heat you can get hot by rocking against each other. **FOR HIM** Unlike some other side-by-side positions, the Crab Embrace allows him to penetrate her easily, and thrust with freedom. If you want even more freedom, move your upper bodies apart (so that you are lying in a wide "V" shape), then she can move her upper thigh as high up his body as possible.

   FOR BOTH To maximize pleasure in Crab Embrace, stroke each other with your fingertips—especially easy-to-reach erogenous zones, such as the buttocks. And keep kissing all the way through. Match the mood of the kiss to the tempo of your lovemaking. Start soft, slow and exploratory, then make your tongue movements increasingly probing and urgent. Wrap your arms around each other and revel in the heat of each other's desire.

It's sensual because ...
you have maximum skin-to-skin contact combined with a deeply satisfying penetration. As you kiss you can hold each other's face or head in your hands for a powerful sense of connection.

Lalatika
and other **erotic embraces**

Like the *Kama Sutra*, the *Ananga Ranga* suggests that lovers should embrace each other in various positions before they start to make love. These "external enjoyments" are designed to develop desire and "divert the mind from coyness and coolness." If you are one to rush straight to sex, it's time to slow down and try some of the following embraces for a more erotic build-up.

Lalatika This is the perfect embrace for couples who are deeply in love and want to show "great endearment" to each other. Stand facing your lover with your arms around each other's waist. Gently touch foreheads, chests, bellies, and thighs (see top-left). Stay perfectly still and enjoy the sensation of having your lover so closely wrapped in your arms. Treat this as a silent, sexy meditation.

Tila-Tandula Try this when you're in a sexy mood but haven't yet taken off your clothes. Simply embrace each other while standing up and press your genitals together: "the *lingam* (penis) should approach the *yoni* (vagina), both being veiled by the dress (see top-right). Avoid interrupting the contact for some time." See if you can arouse each other with words: have a "naughty" chat and feel his erection swell between your bodies as the mood gets hotter.

Jaghan-alingana The passion is mounting in this embrace: he sits on the bed and pulls her onto his lap. Now you abandon yourselves to several minutes of feverish kissing and caressing. Men: remove her underwear while she is on your lap. Put your arms around her body and unclasp her bra. Now take her bra off and lovingly embrace her breasts with your hands and lips (see bottom-left).

Kshiranira He lies on his side in bed and she throws herself down near him, and their limbs then entwine. Lovers should remain like this until "desire is thoroughly aroused in both of you." Hold each other tight and let your bodies move however they want to. Even when you both feel ready for sex, prolong the embrace so that the sexual tension continues to rise (see bottom-right).

Secret
the probing kiss

When you are both aroused and locked in a passionate embrace, try this *Ananga Ranga* kissing technique. Put your hand over your lover's eyes and gently push your tongue into his or her mouth (don't let him or her reciprocate). Now gently explore the mouth with your probing and swirling tongue. Use soft slow movements that are so pleasant they suggest the "higher pleasure" of the penis in the vagina.

building up the **passion**

The Snake Trap

This is a taut and erotic posture in which you both lean back in a sitting position and grasp each other's ankles. The snake in the title refers to his penis, which is "trapped" inside her.

Unlike many other *Ananga Ranga* positions, which allow free and easy movement, this one is designed to be static. Since you are gripping each other's ankles, your erotic movements are limited (of course you can both release each other, but that is not part of the game). **FOR HER** He can flex his penis now and then to give her a jolt of pleasure. **FOR BOTH** Because you are sitting in a face-to-face position you can make time for an extremely sexy conversation. She can begin by telling him how hot it feels to have him inside her.

It's steamy because ...
the trapped position forces you to be inventive. The novel movements you come up with—wriggling, gyrating, penis flexing, or vagina squeezing—feel exciting simply because they are different.

Encircling Position

She sits up in a cross-legged position and then lies on her back. He kneels with his legs wide apart, then leans over her body and uses his hands for support as he gently penetrates her. This is a great position for exhibitionists because she can show herself off from a very titillating angle—think of it as erotic yoga. Meanwhile, the erotic invitation implied by her pose will excite him.

FOR HIM The barrier of her crossed legs means that he can thrust only with the tip of his penis. This means that all the sensations are deliciously concentrated in his glans and his frenulum (the two most sensitive parts of his penis). **FOR HER** The lower third of her vagina (which is her most sensitive part) receives fast, intense, and unrelenting pressure. Emotionally, it can be thrilling because the knotted position of her legs means that she is caught underneath him—if she enjoys feeling submissive and he enjoys feeling dominant, this position can be the perfect turn on for both.

It's steamy because ...

all the erogenous zones in her lower body feel stretched or pressed, so she experiences a rich variety of sensations. And he gets a rush from the wide-open position of her legs.

Intense passion
erotic **skin markings**

The *Ananga Ranga* enthusiastically recommends that lovers use their teeth and nails on each other during foreplay and sex—partly to give each other amazing sensations, but also to leave an erotic mark on the skin. Kalyana Malla believes that there is nothing more delightful to lovers than the skillful use of the nails. The marks left behind are to be cherished as romantic keepsakes.

Sensual scratches The *Ananga Ranga* intended scratches (and bites) to be thrilling and drive lovers to new heights of passion—not to inflict pain. Invite your lover to lie down in bed for a unique type of massage. Instead of using your palms and fingers, use only your fingernails. Make your hands into claw shapes and rake your nails all over your lover's arms, chest, belly, thighs and buttocks. Your touch should be featherlight, and your aim, says the *Ananga Ranga*, is to make your lover's skin tingle, the hair bristle, and a sensual shudder pass over their limbs. If you take you time, this can be part of a massage, which can be revivifying for your lover.

Lightning claw For something wilder, use your nails on your lover when he or she is on top of you during sex. Choose a moment when he or she is not far off orgasm (but not in the final throes), then reach up and scratch your lover quickly along the length of their back with both hands. Don't press too hard (and make sure your fingernails do not have any sharp edges). Your aim is give a sensation that is breathtaking and electrifying. If you get the timing right, it should add to the intensity of the orgasm.

Blissful nibble Like the nails, the teeth—when used correctly— can deliver fantastically exhilarating sensations. Tease your lover by taking his or her toes or the fingertips into your mouth—now gently bite, suck, and nibble. Tell your lover how much you enjoy the taste. Other exquisite nibbling spots include the lower lip, the earlobes, the sensitive site where the shoulders meet the neck, the inner thighs, and the buttocks. Alternatively, try this extremely stimulating

Secret
private messages

Much of the guidance in the *Ananga Ranga* is about teaching lovers how to worship each other's bodies to express their love. If you are in any doubt about scratching or biting your lover's skin, or feel uncomfortable doing this, then don't, since it will then go against the Malla's fundamental message.

If you still want to leave an impression on your lover without scratching or biting, buy a body pen and write a sexy message on your lover's body. Choose somewhere sexy but private such as their inner thigh or just above their pubic triangle. Make your words sweet and loving or suggestive and provocative. Think of it as a gift that will remind them of the special time they spent with you.

leaving the **mark of love**

technique: lick a patch of your lover's skin and then glide or graze your teeth across the wet patch, applying minimal pressure (if unsure, you can practice on the back of your hand first).

Love bruise Leaving a mark on your lover's body is a matter of personal taste (refer to "secret" on page 62 for an alternative). But rather than leaving teeth marks as Kalyana Malla suggests, try sucking your lover's flesh instead. Choose the inner thigh, the arm, or the buttock (a relatively fleshy area), and suck firmly to draw blood to the surface. The *Ananga Ranga* says that the mark you leave will make your lover think of you with a yearning heart, especially if, afterward, you will be spending time apart.

"The peacock's foot or claw is made by placing the thumb upon the nipple, and the four fingers upon the breast adjacent; at the same time pressing the nails till the mark resembles the trail of the peacock walking on mud."

ANANGA RANGA

Ascending Position

The *Ananga Ranga* gives women specific instructions about the Ascending Position. First she should make her lover lie on his back, then she should sit cross-legged on his thighs, seize his penis, and guide it inside her. If she then "moves her waist up and down, advancing and retiring, she will derive great comfort from the process."

FOR HER It is easy for her to have an orgasm in this position, but he can help by sliding his hand between her legs to caress her clitoris. **FOR HIM** There is the raunchier option of her stroking herself while he watches, something that is likely to add to his already heightened state of arousal.

It's raunchy because ... it is all about her pleasure. She can feel him deeply inside her and, if she moves forward or backward, different erotic pressure points are stimulated in her vagina. Meanwhile, he can lie back and relish the sight of her enjoying herself.

"I was lying on the grass on a warm summer's evening when she just squatted on top me, unbuttoned my jeans, and then sat on top of me. **She was in complete control.**"

❝I love the freedom of being on top. **I can concentrate on pleasuring us both**, and can tell from the look on his face that it's one of his favorite positions, too.**❞**

Orgasmic Role Reversal

This is to be performed when the woman is unsatisfied and "still full of the water of love." The *Ananga Ranga* recommends it for times when the man is exhausted and no longer capable of muscular exertion, although today many couples would make it their position of choice. Men and women love woman-on-top positions for their thrilling raunchiness and power to stimulate.

To get into position she straddles his body with her feet flat on the bed and guides him into her. **FOR HIM** She is free to satisfy him in any way she likes. She can bob up and down on his penis, rock back and forth, or squeeze him tight from inside (see pp120-1). **FOR HER** An orgasm is almost guaranteed for her because she is in control of the angle, depth, and pace of penetration.

It's raunchy because ... it gives men the thrill of immediacy. She simply straddles his body and takes him inside her. Then, if she "churns" his penis by making circular motions while moving up and down, he will find the pleasure mind-blowing.

Refined Posture

Sex feels fantastic in this position simply because your bodies fit together so effortlessly. She lies back on the bed with her thighs parted and hips raised and he slips easily inside her. The only taxing part is the effort involved in keeping her body raised. The *Ananga Ranga* has a simple solution for this: the man places a cushion under his lover's lower back to keep her elevated. **FOR BOTH** In doing so he "raises the seat of pleasure" and ensures a "congress that is enjoyed by both."

FOR HER The Refined Posture is a perfect way for him to experiment with different types of thrusting: from slow, smooth strokes that penetrate her deeply, to fast, fleeting strokes that stay shallow. Or a combination of the two. All she needs to do is to lie back and focus on the orgasmic feelings building up inside her.

It's raunchy because ...
the sight of her raised pelvis is an invitation to enter her deeply. The angle also means he can glide in. The impact as he thrusts makes both of you shiver with pleasure. And when she reaches a peak of excitement, she can bump her pelvis against his with each thrust, or tap his bottom with her heel.

Gaping Position

This is an extremely provocative position! He kneels between her legs, nuzzling and licking her inner thighs and clitoris. When she is fully aroused and her body is taut, he pulls back, gets into a kneeling position and swiftly penetrates her. Rather than the comfort of the Refined Posture, the mood of the Gaping Position is tense and yearning. She arches her body up and he grabs her waist so he can be in full possession of her and assert his dominance.

FOR BOTH Make your moves wild and urgent to fuel the raunchy mood. She can take fistfuls of the bed sheet and pull them toward her as she moans with pleasure, or simply undulate and writhe.

It's raunchy because ...

he can plunge deeply in and out without stopping. To add to the intensity, both of you can pant, moan, and gasp. Work up a sweat before you get swept away by the tide of orgasm.

"I love the feeling of being taken in the Gaping Position. There's no other way to describe it: **it makes me weak with desire**—literally!**"**

Pataka
and other **tapping techniques**

The *Ananga Ranga* recommends soft tappings and pattings between couples as a form of "external enjoyment." Kalyana Malla says that these should be mixed up with kisses, nibbles, scratches, embraces, and bites to build up the desire for internal enjoyment or coition. He suggests several different hand techniques for couples to use.

Prasritahasta This means patting with the open palm. Try this before an erotic massage: ask your lover to stand up, then pat your palm across their back and buttocks to invigorate them. Alternatively, your lover can remain lying on their front as you sit astride the backs of their thighs and strike from that position. Massage therapists call this stroke "hacking"—it has a fast stimulating effect and draws blood to the surface. Make all the movements originate from your wrists (your elbows and shoulders should stay still). Several minutes of this will make your lover feel energized and aroused. As in the *Kama Sutra*, the idea behind any kind of tap or spank is not to inflict pain, but to excite your lover so that they are tingling with erotic energy.

Secret
erotic vibrations

The *Ananga Ranga* says that gentle pats to the *yoni* (vagina) are arousing for women. Try giving her a *yoni* massage and alternate your caresses and strokes with pats. Concentrate on the clitoral area and use the flats of your fingers to create gentle vibrations. Ask your lover if she likes the sensations, or be guided by her moans of pleasure.

hitting the spot

Mushti While giving your lover a massage, change your hand position so your fists are lightly clenched and you are striking your lover's body with the fleshy parts on the sides of your hands. The *Ananga Ranga* recommends a soft hammering movement. The change of pressure will arouse your lover. Keep to the muscular areas of your lover's back and buttocks, and avoid the spine.

Sampatahasta This is similar to the "Cobra's Hood" technique (see p21) in the *Kama Sutra*. Hollow your hand slightly and increase the erotic intensity by making your pats slightly harder. If your lover enjoys this, concentrate on the buttocks and start to spank rather than pat. Your aim is to produce stinging or tingling sensations that rouse sexual feelings in your lover.

If you know your lover is turned on by spanking, ask him or her to adopt a much naughtier and more vulnerable position, such as getting down on hands and knees, or lying across your lap, or bending down while holding on to a piece of furniture.

> "Karatadana, as the word denotes, are soft tappings with the hand, by husband or the wife, upon certain members of each other's persons."
> **ANANGA RANGA**

Inverted Embrace

The woman is instructed to "lie straight upon the outstretched person of her lover" and then "apply her breast to his bosom."
FOR HER The *Ananga Ranga* goes on to explain how the woman should get maximum enjoyment from her lover by "moving her hips sharply in several directions." She can move on a horizontal plane too—he can help by grabbing her buttocks or waist and moving her in parallel motion on his body. To assume a more dominating stance, or to steady herself, she can clasp his shoulders.

    FOR BOTH For sheer sexiness, few positions can beat the Inverted Embrace. Both of you experience the high of skin-to-skin contact, plus lots of intense genital friction.

It's passionate because …
she can play a strong, thrusting role. In fact, she can do exactly the movements he would if he were on top. Fast up and down flicks of her pelvis feel pleasurable for her and produce lots of firm friction on her clitoris. In the process, he gets an extremely gratifying penile massage.

❝ Inverted Embrace is my favorite way to reach orgasm. I find a position where the base of **his penis is tight against me**, then I hold on to his shoulders and wriggle and thrust. **❞**

Raised Feet Posture

You can graduate to this position when you are having sex in the missionary position. **FOR HER** As the mood heats up and you want to take your lovemaking to a higher pitch of passion, she can simply raise her legs and rest her feet on the top of his thighs. Her body language simply says: "enter me more deeply."

FOR BOTH Raised Feet Posture is just one of the *Ananga Ranga* positions in which the woman lies beneath the man with her legs raised. Try experimenting to find the leg angle that is most erotic for both of you. Some couples find it exciting if she rests her feet on the backs of his calves and lets her knees fall to the sides. Others love it when she raises her feet as high in the air as possible. For a powerfully intimate moment, she can try wrapping her legs around his body and hugging him close immediately after he climaxes.

It's passionate because ...

he can feel her desire as he presses himself deeply into her. Her knees crush her breasts as he bears down with each thrust—she relishes the force of his body on top of her.

Splitting Position

He is firmly in charge in this position. After placing her on the bed and overwhelming her body with kisses, he kneels between her legs, picks up her ankles, and rests them on his shoulder.

FOR BOTH Because her thighs are close together, you both benefit from a deliciously tight fit as he presses himself inside her.

FOR HER After a gentle start, which gives her vagina time to accommodate him, he begins to thrust faster. Try to feed off each other's erotic energy in this position—work toward a feverish climax. If she needs more clitoral stimulation to make this position truly orgasmic, he can pull out occasionally, take his penis in hand and flick the head quickly up and down on her clitoris before plunging back in.

It's ravishing because ...

he plunges deep inside her; she gasps ecstatically; he thrusts faster and deeper; her moans become louder, and this mood rises to a crescendo until you both experience a heady orgasm.

Placid Embrace

She raises her body into a ramp. Then he slips his hands between her thighs and opens her legs. **FOR HER** He leans in and teases her by nudging her vaginal entrance with the tip of his penis, then, in a swift movement, he enters her fully. She crosses her feet behind his back and surrenders herself to his piston-like moves. If either of you need to shift into something a little less strenuous, he can sit back on his heels and take the weight of her body on his lap.

FOR HIM One of the greatest pleasures of this position is the sight of her body stretched tautly before him. From his vantage point he can admire the shapely curves of her waist and breasts, and also take delight from watching the pleasure on her face.

It's ravishing because ...
he takes firm control as he holds the small of her back and plunges into her—you both get swept away by the emotional intensity of the position. Meanwhile, she gets a head rush from the semi-inverted position, something that she can intensify by letting her head dangle off the edge of the bed.

"Sometimes it's as if **I can't get enough of her.** I grab her by the waist and pull her as close as I can. I love the way she raises her body and gives herself to me.**"**

The world of Tantra
more spicy pleasures from **India**

Thought to have originated in India around 5,000 BCE, Tantric sex has gained much popularity in the West in recent times. In Tantra, lovemaking is seen as a divine act between men and women—an act that should be treated with reverence—and the body is described as a vehicle that can transport its owner to a higher consciousness and state of absolute contentment.

Path to bliss Tantra draws on various practices and techniques, including meditation and yoga, to bring about a state of expanded consciousness or bliss during sensual and sexual interactions.

Tantric sex differs from conventional sex in that couples are in a state of complete immersion as they make love. Instead of being distracted by goals or performance anxieties, they are fully present in the moment, aware only of the erotic sensations.

Oneness Tantric practitioners seek to reach a state of non-thinking ecstasy as they make love by concentrating only on the erotic energy radiating through their bodies. In doing so, they remove any boundaries between themselves and their lover and feel a sense of oneness. In some Tantric disciplines, practitioners avoid having an orgasm during sex, so instead of dissipating erotic energy "outward" they can keep it inside the body, where it is harnessed and used to expand consciousness.

Plenty of other Tantric approaches do include orgasm in their practices, although most recommend that couples don't treat orgasm as the ultimate goal. Once sex becomes goal-orientated with the possibility of success or failure, it stops being truly pleasurable and mindful; instead of enjoying the journey, lovers are focused only on the destination.

Sensory pleasures Beginners in the art of Tantra are taught simple techniques to help them become more fully present in their body and less attached to their thoughts and mental processes. Becoming more aware of your senses is the first step—immersion in the touches, tastes, sounds, smells, and sights of sex can immediately make the experience more sensual and engaging.

Breathing is also important for stilling the mind during Tantric sex. By focusing on your breath and synchronizing it with your lover, you instantly become more present and connected. There are also other more sophisticated breathing techniques in Tantra in which you use your breath to move sexual energy upward through your *chakra* system. (*Chakras* are energy centers that run from the perineum to the crown of the head.)

Practicing Tantric sex can also have a wonderfully positive impact on your general well-being. Tantric practitioners often say that they enjoy an enhanced sense of richness in their everyday experiences.

"In moments of lovemaking, at the climax, the mind becomes empty of thoughts. **For a moment all thoughts disappear**. And this emptiness of mind, this disappearance of thoughts, is the cause of the **showering of divine bliss.**" *FROM SEX TO SUPERCONSCIOUSNESS*

Tantric touch techniques
enhance your **sensual being**

In Tantra, sex is a head-to-toe sensual experience. Instead of focusing just on your lover's genitals, you treat his or her entire body as a single erogenous entity. Your aim is to awaken your lover to the blissful sensations of all-over touch and make him or her remember the old adage that the best things definitely come to those who are prepared to wait.

Keep eyes shut One of the best ways to increase your lover's sensitivity is to ask him or her to close their eyes while you caress the skin (see top-left). The lack of visual distraction makes your lover much more receptive to all the wonderful tactile treats that you offer.

Start by giving your lover a deeply relaxing head or foot massage. If you are giving a head massage, try raking your fingertips softly through the hair for several minutes. Then press your fingertips just above the ears and knead the scalp in firm, slow circles. Next, spread your fingers and thumbs widely apart, then draw them together while pressing down on the scalp.

If you are giving a foot massage, enclose your lover's foot in your warm, oiled hands and hold it firmly. Start to stroke the whole foot in smooth flowing strokes, then push the pad of your thumb in firm caterpillar movements across the sole. Slide your fingers in between each of your lover's toes and then pinch and squeeze each toe.

Touch experiments Now that your lover is relaxed and receptive to your touch, explore different parts of his or her body with your hands. Trace the outline of your lover's face or breasts with your fingertips. Trail your fingers across the chest, belly, legs, or arms. Then start using your mouth. Alternate featherlight kisses with passionate ones on your lover's hands, feet, buttocks, and thighs.

Focus on a particular area: try licking and sucking your lover's earlobes, nipples, fingertips, and toes, then make him or her shiver by blowing cool air across their moist skin. Try to avoid the genital area so that you build up the sense of excitement and anticipation.

Secret
naked exploration

Try this unique Tantric turn-on technique, which is guaranteed not only to build up your desire for each other, but also to amplify feelings of intimacy and trust. Blindfold your lover first, and then yourself. Stand naked before each other and feel your way around each other's bodies using just your hands, lips, and tongue. Imagine you are touching each other for the first time, and revel in the discovery of all the different textures, angles, crevices, and curves of each other's bodies. Whisper about the parts you like touching, and then kiss those sites. When you can no longer contain your excitement, take off your blindfolds and guide each other into bed and make love.

pleasures of the **skin**

Tantric toys Make a Tantric toy box and keep it in your bedroom. Fill it with objects that you can use to give each other amazing sensations during foreplay. For example, you might use silk scarves to waft over the skin, or silk gloves to give a unique and decadent massage. When you're feeling particularly playful, you can use a feather to tickle parts of your lover's body, paying close attention to those erogenous sites such as the breasts, buttocks, and neck (see top-right). Ice is another object you can use to give your lover breathtaking sensations: hold a melting ice cube against her nipples or earlobes, then thrill her by thawing her out with your warm lips and tongue. Devote a whole evening to discovering the types of tactile games that turn your lover on. Your aim is to find the toys and techniques that make them writhe with pleasure.

Remember to keep adding new props to your collection of Tantric toys. Anything that you think might add a frisson of excitement to the pleasures of touching is worth experimenting with.

Scissors

Getting into this position requires concentration and discipline. He lies on his back with his legs apart. She sits between his thighs with her bottom pressed close to his. Then she slips one leg underneath his (and puts her other leg over his waist). She lies back on the bed so her head is at the opposite end to his. In this position she carefully guides his penis into her—his penis is bending in the opposite direction from usual, so all movements should be gentle.

FOR HER Once you are in position, she takes charge of the movement by grinding back and forth. The intense pleasure for her comes from the tight contact between her clitoris and his pubic bone. If she finds the right rhythm and keeps it up, Scissors can yield a powerful orgasm. **FOR HIM** The joy lies in feeling his penis tightly hugged by her vagina. You are unable see each other's faces in Scissors, but you can keep the mood intimate, warm, and connected by holding hands all the way through.

It's sensual because ...
it's the most intimate way possible to just lie back and relax. If you're not holding hands, stroke each other's legs with soft caresses, and communicate your pleasure with moans and sighs.

Yab Yum

This position symbolizes the divine union of Tantric sex. "Yab Yum" means "position of the mother and father." She simply sits in his lap and wraps her feet around his body. It is comfortable, loving, and intimate. By having sex in this position, you let the boundaries between the two of you dissolve.

FOR BOTH From a Tantric point of view, one of the wonderful things about this position is that you can stay in it for a long time. If his erection wanes, it doesn't matter. You can simply hug, kiss, stroke, whisper, and caress until the next wave of arousal comes and sweeps you away.

When he is inside her, focus on the erotic sensations rippling through your body. Rock your pelvises so that his penis moves a little way in and out of her vagina.

It's sensual because ... you can feel the hot glow of desire as you cuddle each other close. Enjoy the beautiful experience of exploring each other with your hands—and make sure you indulge in a long, melting kiss. Get high on the sensations you are sharing.

"We were taught Yab Yum at a Tantric workshop. I loved the fact that my face was nestled between her breasts. **It's a great position for feeling intimate**—both physically and emotionally."

Thigh Press

This position is wonderfully sexy and very easy to get into. He lies on his side while she lies on her back (at right angles to his body), and then she hooks her legs over his.

You can move in different ways in the Thigh Press. He is free to thrust to his heart's content; or she can grind against his body while he stays still; or she can masturbate with him deeply inside her as he moves slowly in and out. **FOR BOTH** It is also a wonderful position for gazing into each other's eyes as you head toward orgasm. For an extra thrill, try the following: take each other repeatedly to the brink of climax, then stop all stimulation and allow the erotic energy to subside. After you have done this a few times, allow yourselves to reach an intense simultaneous orgasm (see p122).

Try doing the Thigh Press near a wall. **FOR HER** Instead of putting her feet on the bed behind his body, she raises her legs in the air and puts her feet on the wall. This braces her body as he thrusts—and makes all the sensations she feels much stronger.

It's steamy because ...

mutual orgasm is more likely, which makes both of you feel extra-aroused. It is easy to experiment with different speeds and techniques for moving. You can also tease each other by varying the pace of your movements.

Rising Sap

This is the erotic version of doing the splits—so she will need a flexible groin and supple thighs. She starts in a conventional woman-on-top position (sitting astride him in a squat) and then parts her thighs in a wide "V" while arching her back. Movement is restricted (although she can do some very sexy undulations), but this doesn't matter because the point of Rising Sap is simply to enjoy the sensation of being joined together. **FOR BOTH** Synchronize your breathing and let the sexual charge build up inside you. When the urge to move consumes you, return to a less demanding woman-on-top position.

It's steamy because ...
it makes her body look very sexy. Her legs are wide open, her thigh muscles are taut and stretched, her breasts look gorgeously touchable, and her neck looks long and graceful. He can feast his eyes on her from below and tell her just how amazing she looks.

❝I absolutely adore watching her when she gets into the Rising Sap position. **I love running my hands along her taut thighs** and working my way up to her breasts.**❞**

Reveal all
the Tantric **art of stripping**

Tantric sex is about stimulating the senses, including sight. Performing a striptease for your lover is the perfect way to start an evening of hot passion because it combines the thrill of exhibitionism with the desire to please your partner. Give your lover a feast for the eyes by removing each item of your clothing slowly and seductively, then finish by offering them your naked body.

Lover's gift If you usually make love in the dark or between the sheets, then it might be time to give your lover a wonderful treat by by offering him or her the opportunity to gaze uninhibitedly at your body. Even if you are very familiar with each other's naked bodies, there is something about the eroticism of stripping that will make your lover really sit up and take in the sight of you.

Enjoy yourself Take your lover into your love chamber (see p12) and ask him or her to lie in bed and watch while you take off your clothes piece by piece. Play some raunchy music as you begin to undress. Rather than following a choreographed set of moves, do what comes naturally. In Tantra, your aim is to immerse yourself totally in sensuality, so do whatever feels good. As you take off your top, for example, drop it on the floor then close your eyes and lightly brush your palms and fingertips over your exposed chest or breasts. Give yourself goosebumps. Trust that your lover will get pleasure from witnessing the fun you are having.

Express yourself When you take off your underwear, enjoy the eroticism of revealing your most intimate parts. Whether you are feeling confident, brazen, liberated, ecstatic, or even timid, make your moves express your mood. It will then feel more natural. For example, women: if you are in an exhibitionist mood, turn your back to your lover, slowly bend over and draw your panties irresistibly slowly over your buttocks. On the other hand, if you're feeling shy, close your eyes, hook your thumbs into the sides of your panties and ease them gradually down as you swirl your hips to the music.

Secret
sweet reflections

If you're shy about stripping, try this lovely Tantric exercise. Stand naked with your lover in front of a full-length mirror and take turns to tell each other which parts of each other's body you love most, and give a reason. Stroke and caress whichever part of your lover's body you're describing at the time. Let your eyes or facial expression radiate admiration. This will boost your lover's self confidence.

Offer yourself When you are completely naked, bask in the feeling of your lover's eyes upon you. Dance however you want to—let your body ripple, sway, or writhe. Find your masculine or feminine energy and express it to the full. Or, if you don't feel like moving, stand still and caress your body with your hands. Close your eyes and get turned on by imagining your hands are those of your lover's. Finally, step up to the bed and offer your gorgeous body to your lover.

Paired Feet

He pulls her body close and he penetrates her easily in this very sexy seated position. **FOR HIM** His hands are free to roam along her thighs, breasts, and belly as you both savor the deep connection.

Make Paired Feet part of a satisfying two-position sequence. You start in the intimate Yab Yum position (see p79), then she turns up the temperature by giving him a slow kiss, and leans back on her hands with his penis still inside her.

FOR BOTH He hugs her knees to his chest and you both thrill each other by contracting and relaxing your love muscles, taking turns so that you feel each other's labor of love. Finally, she raises her legs and puts her feet on his shoulders. He can stay sitting or move into a kneeling position for extra thrusting power. For maximum erotic impact, you can try this sequence on a soft rug in the middle of your candlelit love chamber (see p12).

It's raunchy because …
you can do it on the floor, the sofa, or the bed—wherever you want to. Just close your eyes, throw your head back, and abandon yourself to erotic joy.

" I gave him strict instructions to lie still. Then **I climbed seductively on top**, put him inside me, and **moved wildly** in all directions **"**

Shakti on Top

Shakti was the Hindu goddess who enjoyed a divine erotic union with the Hindu god Shiva. In Tantra the name "Shakti" is often used to refer to all women. Shakti on Top is a position for her to unleash her hot feminine power on him. **FOR HER** She can thrust, grind, wriggle, or vibrate her pelvis on top of him. **FOR HIM** The man benefits from the snug fit created by her closed thighs.

FOR BOTH The raunchiest way to enjoy this position is for her to let go completely and thrill him with uninhibited moans and cries of pleasure. He will soon discover that true abandon is infectious—so expect this position to elicit a lot of noise.

It's raunchy because ...

with every move she can feel the base of his penis rubbing against her clitoris. And his shaft and glans will stimulate all her internal hotspots (including her G-spot) as his penis slides in and out.

Erotic breast massage
celebrate **her softness**

A woman's breasts are revered in Tantra. Tantric sex dedicates an entire massage ritual to women's breasts, a ritual through which a woman, it claims, receives sensual energy from her partner. Breast massage is powerfully arousing for both of you. The practice is also said to generate strong feelings of affection in her because the breasts lie close to the heart.

Express admiration Start by undressing your lover, making sure you do it slowly and lovingly—enjoy the moment when you remove her bra and uncover her breasts. Gaze at them appreciatively and tell her how much you admire them; lean over and kiss each one tenderly before you begin your massage.

Oil trickle Take a bottle of warm, fragrant massage oil, and drizzle it all over her breasts. Let her savor the sensual experience of the oil trickling over her skin, then softly place your hands on her chest. Move your palms in light swirling patterns all over her front—spread the oil evenly over her skin so your hands have a wonderfully slippery surface to glide against. Make the mood loving and intimate by keeping your hands in contact with her body throughout.

Spread erotic sensations Reach forward and glide your hands firmly down the sides of her body, then up along her front, lightly following the contours of her belly and breasts with your palms. Repeat this stroke several times. She will experience a thrill of arousal as your hands brush over her nipples, but don't single her breasts out for special attention just yet. Imagine you are spreading erotic sensations all over the front of her body.

Hands on Once she is fully aroused, pour some fresh oil over her chest, then concentrate on her breasts alone. Make "L" shapes with your hands by pointing your thumbs out at right angles. Sweep your hands up the sides of her breasts, then close your thumbs against your hands and briefly trap her nipples. Try circling your flat palms on top of her breasts so they just graze her nipples.

Secret
spread the joy

Women can boost their pleasure during a breast massage with the following Tantric visualization: each time you inhale, imagine that you are pulling hot erotic energy from your breasts down to your stomach and then to your genitals. Feel the warm, tingling, and melting sensations spreading through your clitoris and vagina on each inward breath and harness it.

It might help to visualize the energy as the color red. Start to move your body as the pleasure starts spreading—arch your back or ripple your pelvis, or lean back and feel the heat of your lover's body mingling with yours.

enraptured by your lover's **touch**

Peak moments Turn your attention to her nipples and make your touch firmer and more urgent—tweak and pinch her nipples. Try scissoring one of her nipples between your index finger and middle finger, then use a finger of your other hand to rapidly brush or flick the tip. Do the same to her other breast.

Complete your massage by kneeling beside her body and taking her nipples in your mouth. Suck them, then pull away and blow on them. Graze them with your teeth. Finally, lie gently on top of her and kiss her on the mouth while you touch your nipples to hers.

"Feel the fine qualities of creativity permeating your breasts and assuming delicate configurations." *SHIVA SUTRA*

At one with nature

passion under **the stars**

There is something not only playful, but sensual and exhilarating about making love outdoors, especially on a warm summer's evening. In Tantric terms, it allows you to get into a blissfully relaxed state, to be at one with your lover, and to connect deeply with nature.

Choose the perfect site Find a beautiful spot with your lover where you can lie down and gaze at the fluttering leaves of a tree or the clouds in the sky. If it is nighttime, choose a secluded place far away from the sounds of civilization, where you can appreciate the wondrous enormity of the night sky dotted with stars.

Meditate in nature Spread a blanket on the ground and lie down on your back with your arm around your lover and your bodies close together. Breathe in time with each other and meditate silently on everything around you: the smells of the earth, the heady aroma of the flowers and plants; the solidity of the ground supporting you; the temperature of the air against your skin; the gentle pressure of your lover's hand; the deep azure—or black— of the sky. Be receptive to the sounds of nature around you, too.

Feel your body begin to relax and your mind expand as you connect with nature. Imagine that you are part of the environment, rather than being something separate from it. Stroke each other softly; let your breathing patterns synchronize and imagine all the boundaries between you and your lover dissolving.

Share a kiss When you are both in a blissful state of relaxation, turn to each other and lose yourself in a long, passionate kiss. Stay tuned in to your senses. Immerse yourself in the sensations of every touch and taste of the kiss. Be mindful of the smallest interactions between you. Let arousal build within your body and flow through you. If you can, take off your clothes and enjoy being naked together. Hold your lover close and continue to breathe in time with them. Let desire ripple through you before you finally make love.

Secret

vacation romance

Be adventurous! Choose a romantic and picturesque location while you are away on vacation, and make love outdoors: try an idyllic beach, a hillside, a mountaintop, a forest, or the ocean. For a truly inspired thrill, have sex outside during a raging thunderstorm. (But always be mindful of local laws, since this may be illegal.) Minimize any risk of being discovered by being extremely discreet: for example, lie in spoons position under a blanket, and rather than in-and-out thrusts, rely on small movements and muscle contractions (see pp44, 120).

Women: dress in a flowing skirt without any underwear. Once you have found your spot, whisper in his ear your naughty secret. It will drive him wild with desire.

The Diamond

This feels excitingly experimental: her legs are open wide, but her feet are together in a diamond shape. He is on top but the barrier of her legs keeps him at a distance.

The sensation of being completely open to him makes her feel submissive and vulnerable. Meanwhile, he is titillated by the unimpeded view of her genitals and excited by the prospect of penetrating her deeply.

Try this position at the peak of passion.

FOR HIM He can maximize sensation by relaxing his buttocks as he thrusts (men typically tense up when they are on top and this can stop the free flow of sexual energy).

FOR HER She can heighten her pleasure by relaxing her thighs, while pleasuring herself if she wants extra stimulation. Concentrating on the build up of erotic sensation in your genitals will help both of you to reach orgasm.

It's passionate because ...

both of you are excited by the novelty of the position. Her wide-open pose inspires him to move with abandon. Meanwhile, she has easy access to her clitoris and can stimulate herself to a red-hot orgasm.

❝She sat on my lap **cuddling and kissing** me, then she just lay back on the bed, asked me to hold her feet, and gave herself to me. **I've rarely had such an intense orgasm.❞**

Parallel Motion

FOR HER She lies back on his lap and he guides her onto his erection, giving her a feeling of being wonderfully filled. From now on movement is limited, which is fine if you simply want to relish the sensation of being joined together. For a more passionate encounter, try rubbing massage oil into your bodies beforehand, particularly the backs of her thighs and her buttocks, and the fronts of his thighs and his stomach. **FOR HIM** If you are both slippery with oil, he will be able to move her in a back and forth parallel motion on his lap. Or you can forget about any kind of disciplined movement and just have sexy fun slipping and sliding against each other.

It's passionate because ...

he glides slickly in and out with increasing speed. The erotic tempo gets faster and more furious by the second. He can add to the intensity of the mood by pressing his fingers against her clitoris.

Blissful *lingam* and *yoni* massage
The art of **hand pleasure**

In Tantric sex there are no goals and no pressure to reach orgasm. You should not be under any time constraints either. This means that when you receive a genital massage, you are free to lie back, relax, and simply float on waves of bliss as your lover touches, caresses, and strokes you.

Worship the body Tantric massage is a way of honoring and revering your lover's body. Center yourself before you give a massage: take a few long deep breaths and focus on the air flowing freely in and out of your body as you breathe. Men should treat this as a chance to be deeply affectionate as they pleasure their partner.

Caressing her Rub some massage oil between your palms. Now rest one palm flat against her vagina—the gentle pressure will instantly focus her attention on the site. Begin to stroke the whole of her vagina in smooth strokes (from the back to the front). This soothingly erotic movement will both relax and pleasure her.

As she becomes more aroused, start to apply greater pressure with your fingertips on each palm stroke. Let them follow the natural contours of her vulva, dipping fleetingly into her vagina and circling her clitoral hood. Gradually change your stroke so that you are using just the tip of your index finger—move it in slow circles from her vagina to her clitoris and back again, varying the pressure as you go.

When your lover is fully lubricated, slide your index and middle finger into her vagina. Glide your fingers in and out, and maintain a regular pace. Use your other hand to stimulate her clitoris. Find the stroke that she most enjoys: try tickling the head with your fingertip, or rub your finger in circles on her clitoral hood. Ask your lover to breathe deeply and to imagine all the erotic feelings in her vagina expanding outward and rippling throughout her whole body.

> **"** Behold the Shiva lingam… firm as the Himalaya mountain, tender as a folded leaf…**"**
> *LINGA PURANA*

Caressing him Position your lover's penis so that it points toward his head, then place your warm, oiled hand on top so that your fingertips are reaching toward his testicles. Start to stroke his shaft from bottom to top using enough hand pressure to make the skin of his penis feel pleasantly stretched.

Now increase his erotic pleasure by extending your hand strokes to include his perineum and testicles. Vary the pressure of your hands as they travel: firm fingertip pressure on his perineum; a light tickling pressure on his testicles; and firm palm pressure on his shaft.

Gradually start to pay more attention to his shaft, touching every part of it: try a delicate pitter-pattering movement with your fingertips. Or stroke up and down the shaft and glans with one oiled fingertip. Tease him like this for a minute or two. Then enclose his penis between your interlinked hands so that the pads of your thumbs rest on his frenulum (the sensitive band of tissue on the underside of his glans). Slide your hands slowly and firmly up and down, and enjoy his responses to this incredibly erotic stroke.

As your lover's arousal intensifies, ask him to breathe deeply and to imagine that each breath is sweeping powerful erotic sensations up through his whole body.

Secret
loving energy
If you feel yourself getting turned on as you massage your lover, meditate on the sensations in your genitals. Imagine that you can pull them up through your heart and transform them into loving energy. Let this loving energy flow down through your arms and fingertips into your lover's body.

Union of Love

The secret power of this sex position lies in her feet and her legs. **FOR HIM** Because she is squatting astride him, she can use her thigh power to bounce on him until he orgasms. And when her thighs or her knees get tired, she can put her knees on the floor and thrill both of you with rapid pelvic thrusts.

FOR HER Treat Union of Love as a way for her to expend all her sexual energy on him. Not just in bounces and thrusts, but in wild kisses and feverish caresses too. She is in control throughout.

When you are both satiated she can sit on his lap with her forehead pressed to his. This is a wonderful position to enjoy some Tantric "afterplay": gently stroke each other with your fingertips while breathing in time with each other. Let your breath mingle and become slower and quieter, as you slowly descend from the erotic high. Bask in the joy of being joined so intimately.

It's ravishing because ... he has sensation overload on the front of his body. Her lips brush against his lips; her breasts and nipples graze his chest; and her vagina massages his penis. She enjoys being in control as she drives him toward an overwhelming orgasm.

"The Union of Love turns me on like no other position This is because I dictate the pace and rhythm, which means I can **bring myself to orgasm** every single time."

Lighting the Lamp

He lies on his side while she lies on her back and hooks one leg over his body. Since your bodies are wide apart you can both move at a frenetic pace in Lighting the Lamp. He can thrust and she can vibrate her hips. Both of you are free to use your hands, too; on yourselves or on each other. Alternatively, you can grip each other's hands.

Since you are facing in opposite directions, you cannot easily see each other's expressions—instead close your eyes and listen to each other's moans and gasps. **FOR BOTH** Try communicating by squeezing, scratching, or rubbing each other. This is a great non-verbal way to speed up the tempo of your lovemaking. For example, the faster she rubs her hand on his thigh, the faster she wants him to thrust. Pace yourselves so you reach orgasm at the same time (see p122 about techniques to orgasm simultaneously).

It's ravishing because …
you both have the freedom to make your movements fast and wild. Make this your final position after some slow and sensual lovemaking, and take the chance to free yourselves of all restraint.

Animal sex
unleash **your wild side**

Tantric sex is usually perceived to be quiet, still, and sensual, with an emphasis on establishing a deep connection with your partner. Yet it can also be the opposite: noisy, wild, and primal. The important part of Tantra is that you get more connected with the present.

Raucous focus Moving wildly and making lots of noise can get you into a meditative state just as effectively as a quieter ritual. This is because it distracts the mind and helps to still your thoughts.

Serpent power Unleashing a type of energy called *kundalini* (or serpent power) is a traditional Tantric practice that's great fun to do. To activate *kundalini* with your lover, put on some fast, rhythmic music and stand opposite each other. Start shaking your bodies. Begin with your knees, then include your hips and belly. Gradually let the shaking take over your whole body. Imagine you are standing on a platform that is vibrating uncontrollably. Smile or laugh with your lover if it feels funny. Enjoy the feeling of energy surging up your body. Keep going until you feel charged and exhilarated.

Heavy panting Now face each other, stick your tongue out as far as you can and pant like a dog. If you feel silly, stop and laugh, and then continue. Every time you exhale, draw your abdomen in so you push out all the air. Keep doing this for as long as you can (but stop if you feel dizzy). At the end you will feel energized, but relaxed also.

Animal positions After shaking your body and panting heavily, you should feel open, invigorated, and completely free with each other. Capitalize on these feelings by having sex—ignore all your usual inhibitions and go completely wild. Start by getting down on all fours and let your lust dictate you. For example, play fight; get behind your lover; kiss them hungrily and passionately; bite each other. When you're both completely aroused, surrender to rampant no-holds-barred sex in any position that feels primitive, ravishing, and animalistic. And, finally, make as much noise as you want.

Secret
wild dancing

Tantric teachers recommend wild dancing to help you get in touch with your animal nature and lose your inhibitions. Put some music on—something rhythmic that makes you and your lover want to dance. Close your eyes and visualize a predatory animal: a panther, a snake, or an eagle, for example. Now start to move like the animal and feel its carnal spirit.

❝... get involved in it, in your totality ... Become non-thinking. Only then does the awareness happen that you have become one with someone.**❞** *OSHO, THE BOOK OF SECRETS*

untamed **play**

sultry pleasures
from
Arabia

"The man who deserves favors is, in the eyes of women, the one who is anxious to please them." *THE PERFUMED GARDEN*

Sultry pleasures from Arabia
the world of *The Perfumed Garden*

Picture a decadent Bedouin tent made from colored brocade, decorated with silk, filled with exotic perfumes, and illuminated by flickering candlelight. Inside the tent is a throne on which the man sits waiting for his lover … this is the kind of heady and sultry atmosphere that Sheikh Nefzawi, author of *The Perfumed Garden*, wanted lovers to experience in their lovemaking.

New insights It was in 15th-century Tunis—one of the grandest and richest parts of the Ottoman Empire, famous for its architecture and dedication to learning—that Sheikh Nefzawi wrote *The Perfumed Garden*. His intention behind writing the book was to share erotic insights with men, so that they and their wives would experience maximum enjoyment during sex. He described sex as "man's highest pleasure."

Adventurous positions Like other erotic classics, *The Perfumed Garden* features a gorgeous array of sex positions. Some of them are inspired variations on the missionary position, while others are wildly extravagant, and some even involve props. For example, in a position called The Stab with a Lance, the woman hangs from the ceiling on cords while the man "positions his member opposite her vagina." The man then swings the woman back and forth, taking pleasure in the rhythmic manner in which their genitals keep meeting, until he ejaculates.

The Sheikh admits that positions such as The Stab with a Lance are more likely to be the stuff of erotic imaginings rather than real-life sex. Some of the Sheikh's more achievable—and most pleasurable—sex positions are featured in this book.

Private parts As well as suggesting a variety of sex positions, the Sheikh speaks lyrically about the male and female genitals, even giving names to the different types he identified. He used the moniker the "ever ready" for one of his favorite types of vagina: one that is passionately fond of the virile member. He wrote: "It is neither frightened nor ashamed when someone raises the clothes that cover it … and it gives the member the warmest welcome".

The Sheikh is equally fascinated in the male genitals, naming almost 40 different types—for example, the "untameable" (when it is swollen and erect, it starts to move its head looking for the vagina, which it then enters brusquely); the "quencher" (thick, strong, and slow to ejaculate); and the "searcher" (which penetrates unusual places).

The romantic idealist For all his objective descriptions of sex positions and forensic listing of genital types, the Sheikh does appear to have been something of a romantic idealist. He believed that passionate sex was the result of ardent love and wrote that when a man is intensely in love, "all the pleasures of coition become easy for him."

"The hearts of those who love and are separated from the object of their love, make **their hearts burn with love's fire** ... they suffer under the vicissitudes of their passion, and all this as a consequence of their burning desire for contact.**"** *THE PERFUMED GARDEN*

Getting intimate

the Sheikh's guide to a **woman's body**

Sheikh Nefzawi devotes the beginning of *The Perfumed Garden* to a rapturous description of feminine beauty. In line with Arabic tastes of the time, the Sheikh's ideal woman was shapely and Rubenesque, with "admirable flanks, majestic thighs, and nobly planned buttocks." For this reason, the way a woman dressed and the make-up she wore were considered extremely important.

Feminine beauty As a supreme admirer of the female form, the Sheikh recommended that women should emphasize their natural assets. In particular, a woman should dress in such a way that "when she walks her natural parts stand out under her clothing". He also described his idea of bodily perfection from head to toe:

Kissable lips Sheikh Nefzawi recognized the powerful sex appeal of a woman's lips. He specified that her mouth should be graceful and her lips vermilion. Women: to create a gorgeously kissable mouth, use a lip pencil to emphasize the curves of your lips and the sexy lines of your cupid's bow. Then paint your lips with a vibrant red lipstick. Drink plenty of water to keep your lips plump and soft.

Curvy body Go to bed wearing the sexiest, most decadent corset you can find—one that complements your figure perfectly and draws your lover's eye to the feminine swell of your hips and breasts, as well as the way your waist nips in. If you are not particularly well-endowed in the bust region, wear a balcony corset that pushes your breasts up and invites your lover to gaze longingly at them.

Sexy navel The ideal belly is described as "gently domed" and graced with a "deep and sunken" navel—one of the most neglected erotic zones of the female body. Draw your lover's eye to your navel by decorating it with a temporary tattoo, a pattern drawn in body paint, or some stunning jewelry. Alternatively, make a "honey pot." Drizzle honey into your navel, then invite your lover to taste you.

Elegant legs Maximize the appeal of your legs by making them touchably smooth and hairless. If you have beautifully tanned skin,

Secret

adore her curves

The Perfumed Garden constantly reminds men that the sexiest lovers were those who wanted to please women. So next time you are sharing a private moment with your lover, tell her how much you appreciate her curves.

Stand behind her when she is naked and run your hands sensually over her waist and hips. Nuzzle your face in the place where her neck meets her shoulder and brush her skin with your lips. Then smooth your palms up over her belly and gently cup her breasts in your hands.

Try doing this in front of a full-length mirror so that she can watch your hands stroking her most feminine parts. Let her know how arousing you find her body. This will do wonders for your love life.

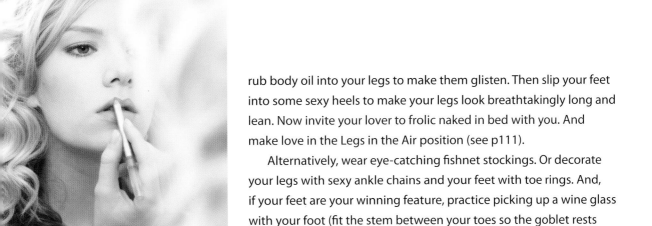

rub body oil into your legs to make them glisten. Then slip your feet into some sexy heels to make your legs look breathtakingly long and lean. Now invite your lover to frolic naked in bed with you. And make love in the Legs in the Air position (see p111).

Alternatively, wear eye-catching fishnet stockings. Or decorate your legs with sexy ankle chains and your feet with toe rings. And, if your feet are your winning feature, practice picking up a wine glass with your foot (fit the stem between your toes so the goblet rests on the top of your foot) and passing it to your lover.

celebrate **your beauty**

❝Let praise be given to God that he has created woman with her beauty and appetizing flesh; that he has endowed her with hair, waist, and throat, breasts which swell, and amorous gestures that increase desire.**❞ *THE PERFUMED GARDEN***

Eleventh Posture

Many couples say that this sensual "missionary" position is their favorite way to make love. Once he has penetrated her, he can support himself on his hands or his forearms. If he supports himself on his hands in a push-up position, there is space between both partners, and he can thrust using his whole body. **FOR HIM** If he rests on his forearms, sex becomes closer and more intimate. Although space is a little more restricted, he can still perform wild pelvic thrusts.

There is a small but powerfully effective technique that increases women's pleasure in the Eleventh Posture. It is called "riding high" and involves him pushing his body up along hers. So, for example, if his nipples are opposite hers, he inches his body up slightly higher so that his nipples are above hers. **FOR HER** This has the exciting effect of pushing the shaft of his penis very tightly against her clitoris, creating more erotic friction with each thrust.

It's sensual because ...

unlike positions from some of the Indian erotic texts, it does not demand contortions or a high level of flexibility. Instead, you can relax comfortably into it and focus exclusively on enjoying erotic pleasure. You can also make the most of the emotional intimacy of being face to face.

Love's Fusion

This is just a roll away from the Eleventh Posture (see opposite). He holds her tight and turns so that he is positioned on his side. Her body partially follows his, so she is half on her back and half on her side with her thigh hooked over his hip, which takes the weight off her body. **FOR BOTH** The change of position turns the erotic mood from one of male dominance to something more equal. *The Perfumed Garden* states: "the woman can help, if she likes, to make the necessary movements." Love's Fusion is fantastically versatile. It is easy, for example, to roll a bit further so that you are both lying on your sides facing each other. Then, if she wants to be the more dominant one, she can push him onto his back and climb on top.

It's sensual because ...

he cradles her by placing one arm around her shoulders and the other on her buttock. She feels completely held. Their faces are close so both partners can lightly touch lips and feel the seductive heat of each other's breath. She can run her fingers through his hair or lovingly cup his face in her hands.

"It's exciting to experiment with different positions, but we always find ourselves returning to the classic missionary or Love's Fusion because **our bodies fit so naturally."**

Playful frolics
Arabian **seduction techniques**

"See that you frolic before making love" is one of the sexiest pieces of advice that Sheikh Nefzawi offers to lovers in *The Perfumed Garden*. By first exploring each other with your hands, lips, and tongues, you will be deeply aroused when you eventually make love. This will intensify the orgasms you have and lead to an incredibly fulfilling lovemaking experience.

Fingertip tour Take turns trying this simple but incredibly sexy technique on each other. Ask your lover to lie naked on the bed and lightly trail your fingertips all over the front of his or her body—make your touch incredibly light so that your fingertips are barely grazing the skin. (If your lover is ticklish, increase the pressure, then reduce it again when you sense that he or she is becoming more relaxed.) As the erotic atmosphere builds, let your fingertips stray to your lover's genitals and nipples and other erogenous sites, but then pull them away again. Keep teasing your lover with this "give and take away" type of touch until your lover is ravenous for you.

A trail of kisses Soft kisses and nibbles are much loved by Sheikh Nefzawi, particularly on the inner thighs. Start by kissing your lover's toes and the soles of the feet, then slowly work your way up the calves leaving a trail of featherlight kisses. As you move up to the thighs, make your kisses stronger and more stimulating—swirl your tongue on the skin, and suck the flesh into your mouth, grazing it with your teeth. Look up every now and then to make erotic eye contact with your lover.

Focus your kisses on the inner thighs, swapping frequently from one to the other, so that you can briefly caress your lover's genitals on your way past. Use a light, teasing touch with your lips or tongue—or just get close and tantalize your partner with a hot breath. Do not give your lover oral sex until he or she is completely aroused. Then indulge your partner with mouth and tongue strokes that lead to orgasm. (See page 28 for more on oral sex techniques.)

Secret
the hand of love
While you are busy caressing your lover with your lips and tongue, rest your hand on one of your lover's hotspots. As Sheikh Nefzawi says: "lay a provoking hand upon her pubes" (or buttocks, belly, breasts, or thighs). The subtext is: "This is the place I will kiss you next".

"If you do not animate her with your frolics and kisses, with nibblings of her thighs and close embraces, you will not obtain what you desire; you will experience no pleasure when she shares your couch, and she will feel no affection for you.**"**
THE PERFUMED GARDEN

"Place in the tent golden cassolettes filled with perfumes, such as green aloes, ambergris, nedde, and other pleasant odors ... when she inhales the perfumes, she will be delighted, all her joints will slacken, and she will swoon away."

THE PERFUMED GARDEN

breathe in the aroma of **passion** ...

Sexy scents
the power of **fragrance**

A gorgeous fragrance can have a profound effect on your lovemaking. The right scent has the power to excite sexual desire in both men and women. The response is natural and, in fact, wearing the right perfume, says Sheikh Nefzawi, can stir your lover's lust so much that he or she loses any inhibitions, relaxes, and then surrenders to you completely.

Secret
scent tour

The Perfumed Garden is all about experimenting and discovering as many erotic pleasures as possible. Try this one: invite your lover to go on a sensual scent tour of your body. Dab some perfume in a secret place and challenge your lover to discover where it is.

Good spots to put your special fragrance include the nape of the neck (especially if you have got long hair that needs to be lifted up), the backs of the knees, the inner thighs, or the navel.

You should both be naked, and, for a slightly kinky touch, put a blindfold on your lover—not being able to see will enhance the sense of smell, too. The scent tour is both exciting and playful, and can result in an extended spell of foreplay.

Your secret perfume Find a stunning scent that you both adore—then wear it only to bed and on no other occasion. In time, both you and your lover will come to associate that fragrance exclusively with intimacy and lovemaking. Ultimately, you will find yourself becoming aroused at the first whiff, even before you have had a chance to touch or kiss. Choose a perfume that is bold and provocative with spicy, woody, or oriental notes that conjure up images of heat and passion. In particular, look for amber, sandalwood, cinnamon, cloves, nutmeg, and cedar. If you and your lover are going to be apart, give your partner a piece of your underwear sprayed with your "love" fragrance as an erotic keepsake.

Fragrance chamber Borrow a technique from *The Perfumed Garden*: fill your bedroom with intoxicating scents, then invite your lover in for a gloriously sensual seduction routine. Lighting scented candles, displaying bunches of flowers, or sprinkling fresh petals are wonderful ways to fragrance a room, but for the most redolent aroma, nothing can beat using essential oils in an oil burner. Choose heady varieties such as ylang ylang, jasmine, or sandalwood; or combine a number of oils to make a sexy signature scent.

For an especially decadent treat, prepare a sensual bath for your lover: fill the tub with hot water, then add a few drops of your lover's favorite essential oil and sprinkle the bath water with rose petals. Place lighted candles all around the bath and invite your lover in. Shut the door behind you to trap the hot steamy fragrance inside and then inhale all the heady scents as you bathe together.

Frog Fashion

To get into this sexy sitting position, she lies back on the bed and brings her knees to her chest and her heels to her buttocks. Then *The Perfumed Garden* instructs the man to "seat himself in front of the woman's vulva, (pull her toward him) and introduce his member." **FOR HER** She can enjoy being pleasured because, by sitting in this manner, he can experiment with his hand positioning and discover how she most likes to be touched.

Because he is sitting down, his movements are limited. Fortunately, she can compensate by drawing him closer with her hands, and wiggling and shaking her hips. When he is approaching the point of no return, *The Perfumed Garden* recommends that the man grasp the woman's upper arms and draw her as close as possible for the propitious moment. **FOR BOTH** This brings you both into a steamy sitting-up position in which you strain erotically against one another, and engage in eye contact.

It's steamy because ...
her wiggling moves feel sharply stimulating for both partners. And you can look into each other's eyes and see the arousal levels soar. To make this position even steamier, try it while you are having a hot, luxurious bath together. Not many sex positions work in the bath; this is one of the few that does.

Legs in the Air

In this incredibly erotic pose, he starts by kneeling before her, then slowly and teasingly, she raises one leg and rests it along the front of his body.

FOR HIM He has a few seconds to take in the sight of her naked body as she lies with her legs wide open, then she raises the other leg, too. Now both of her legs rest on one of his shoulders. As he enters her, he moves into an upright kneeling position and leans his body against her legs, which are pointing straight in the air. He can use one of his hands to gently caress her breasts.

FOR HER If she likes, he can take her ankles in his hands, and push them down toward her body as he thrusts inside her. If this is too intense, she can bend her knees a little, which he can cradle to his chest for support. His thrusting moves should be small, sharp, and shallow.

It's steamy because ... her gorgeous legs take center stage. She feels hot and sexy and he feels fantastically aroused by the look and feel of her silky calves and thighs. To make the Legs in the Air move even more provocative, she can wear stockings and heels.

"I absolutely adore my girlfriend's long and smooth legs. In this position I get to hold and caress them as I make love to her."

Aphrodisiac foods
prepare a **bedtime feast**

Some foods are suggestive in shape, and many have arousing aromas or feel sensual on the tongue. *The Perfumed Garden* rightly emphasizes the connection between food and sex, and claims that eating the right foods is the way to ensure sexual prowess in both sexes. For example, a man who drinks camel's milk and honey will "keep the member in erection day and night."

Sexy menu Sharing the right food can be one of the most sensual ways to get in the mood for a long night of passion. Try taking some sexy tidbits to bed and lovingly feed each other. Pick foods that titillate your tongue, smell irresistible, or—like oysters—just make you think of sex and romance.

The fruits of passion Try blindfolding your lover and teasing a series of fruity treats, such as raspberries and pieces of plum and mango, into his or her mouth. Let your fingers linger on the lips and ask your lover to savor the taste and texture. Then hold a grape between your lips and softly kiss it into your lover's mouth for a heightened moment of intimacy.

Tiny pieces of fruit are also perfect to eat off your lover's body. Arrange a winding trail of pomegranate seeds or grape halves from the chest to the genitals. Make your lover tingle with anticipation by eating them very slowly, always from north to south.

Soft and creamy Cold foods, such as ice cream, are ideal for sensual play. Honor the tradition of feeding each other ice cream in bed, but make sure you "accidentally" drop some on each other's naked flesh. A cold shock followed by the feel of a warm, wet tongue caressing the skin can be electrifying, especially on erogenous parts of the body, such as the neck and the nipples.

Alternatively, drizzle cream over the front of your lover's body. Make your lover close his or her eyes while you slide a cream-coated finger between the lips. Once you have teased the taste buds, pour the cream provocatively over your lover's belly—let it pool in the navel.

Secret
fruit of passion

Why not try your hand at making your very own love elixir that is guaranteed to end up with both of you drinking it in bed?

Start by inventing a deliciously potent "love potion" together (make sure you give it a suitably provocative name). Have fun in the kitchen as you make your drink together. Dab a little on the end of your lover's nose and lick it off, and then lick your lover's neck or earlobe with the cold tip of your tongue.

Once you have made the drink, pour it into a glass and decorate it with a plump cherry on a stem. Take turns sipping the cocktail until the glass is empty. Now take the cherry stem in your teeth and invite your lover to take a bite of the cherry as you dangle it mischievously between his or her lips.

foods of **love**

Now dip the tip of your tongue in, swirling it around the navel first, and moan with pleasure as you lick off every last drop.
Sticky and messy Being covered in sticky stuff makes even the most grown-up lovers appreciate the joys of messy play. It just feels silly, naughty, and a little wild. Try smothering each other in honey, syrup, or chocolate sauce, then begin ravishing each other. Abandon yourselves to pleasure: kiss and lick your way to orgasm, or just writhe around laughing and having fun.

"He who will boil some asparagus and then fry it in fat, adding some yolks and powdered condiments … will find his desires and powers considerably strengthened."
THE PERFUMED GARDEN

Lip love
intoxicating **kissing techniques**

Kissing is the most erotic act of all—it heightens arousal and makes you feel extremely connected to each other. A hot kiss can instantly put you in the mood for sex by making you fizz with lust. *The Perfumed Garden* recommends kissing, nibbling, and the sucking of each other's lips as an essential foreplay technique, and as a way of building "durable affection" between a couple.

Mood kisses Match your kissing technique to your mood. If you are feeling extremely turned on, kiss each other with frenzied passion; push your tongue deeply into your lover's mouth and kiss with insatiable intent. If the mood is tender and romantic, cup your lover's face in your hands, gaze into his or her eyes, then close your eyes and press your parted lips softly to your lover's. If you are feeling sensual, explore your lover's mouth with a slow exploratory tongue, then increase the tempo of the kiss as things get hotter.

When you are feeling experimental, test some new techniques on each other. Suck the tip of your lover's tongue or the lower lip during a kiss—this feels naughtily reminiscent of oral sex. Run the tip of your tongue along the inside of the lips. And then try "piercing" your lover's closed lips with the point of your tongue.

Intensify the act For novel sensations, try kissing your lover after drinking an ice-cold drink. The combination of your cool and warm tongues twining around each other will feel amazingly sexy. Plus, you could surprise your lover by pushing an ice cube into his or her mouth as you kiss—see how quickly you can make it melt by pushing it back and forth between your mouths.

Secret
crazy kiss

As *The Perfumed Garden* recommends, use a kiss to show your lover just how much you want them—right here, right now! Make known your feelings of unquenchable desire by pushing your lover against a wall to plant a kiss. It does not matter whether you are in private, or in public.

Press your hips against your lover and slide your hands around his or her back. Take control by clasping the buttocks. A wall provides useful support if you want to slide down your lover's body to deliver explosive oral sex straight after.

❝The most delightful kiss is that which is planted on moist ardent lips, and accompanied with suction of the lips and tongue, so that the emission of a sweet intoxicating saliva is produced.**❞** *THE PERFUMED GARDEN*

Race of the Member

Many classic Eastern sex positions specify that the woman should lie on her back with her knees raised. Race of the Member reverses this advice completely: the man adopts the "feminine" position while his lover gets to ride him.

FOR HIM To get into position, *The Perfumed Garden* suggests the man should lie down, raise his knees in the air, and make sure his buttocks remain on the floor. **FOR HER** The woman then sits in the saddle formed by his legs and chest and takes his member inside her. Now she can grind or bob up and down on him. There is also a more advanced technique lovers can try in Race of the Member: she puts her knees on the floor and grasps her lover's shoulders with her hands, then the man moves her with his thighs.

It's raunchy because …

he experiences the thrill of submission and she enjoys the excitement of domination. *The Perfumed Garden* recommends that the woman seats herself on her lover "as if on horseback" and then, quite literally, rides him.

Driving the Peg Home

This is the perfect position for a quickie. There is no sensual build-up, but simply a primal urge to have each other immediately. He simply picks her up and takes her against the wall, so she is "hanging" on his "peg." **FOR BOTH** Try this position when you are both hungry for sex, perhaps when you have been apart for a while and want an incredibly hot reunion. Or try it if you usually have sex that is tender and sensual, and you would like to shake up your sex life with something more wild and naughty. Combine it with lots of feverish kisses.

To heighten the sense of the illicit, try it in a semi-public place where you can fantasize about being discovered. It will give you a frisson of anxiety that will raise your arousal levels much higher.

It's raunchy because ... it feels very raw, as lovers express to each other their overwhelming lust. He is excited by the immediacy of picking her up and penetrating her. She is thrilled by the force of his desire and by his physical strength as he lifts her into his arms.

"Having sex standing up is such a turn-on and gives me an **amazing erotic thrill**. I feel so excited to know he has to have me immediately and **I love the way he grabs me."**

Fitting on of the Sock

The Perfumed Garden gives explicit instructions about how a man should build up the woman's pleasure one erotic step at a time. First, he should sit between her legs and grasp his member using his thumb and forefinger. Next, he should push his member between the lips of her vulva. **FOR HER** He rubs the woman with his penis "until her vulva is moist with the liquid that escapes from it." Finally, having made her weak with pleasure, he penetrates her fully.

FOR HIM This sudden change of pace as he enters her and starts thrusting can feel wildly exciting. If he wants to prolong sex in this raunchy position, he should pull out at any stage and thrill his lover with the opening moves all over again.

It's raunchy because ...

the way he uses his penis to tease her slowly raises her arousal to an extraordinary level. The stimulation of her clitoris by the tip of his penis gives her direct, perfectly targeted pleasure. And the friction on his glans is extremely arousing for him too, not to mention the sight of her writhing in pleasure.

"He **strokes and teases** me with the tip of his penis—then he suddenly pushes in deep. **It makes me gasp every time."**

Tenth Posture

To perform this position in the spirit that Sheikh Nefzawi intended, you need something to hold on to, such as the back of a sofa or a headboard, which will act as a shock absorber during wild and rampant sex. To get into position, she leans back and grips the headboard behind her, while arching her pelvis upward to meet him. He penetrates her while holding on to the headboard, too. **FOR BOTH** The only other instruction *The Perfumed Garden* offers is: "when you begin to work, let your movements keep time"—by doing so, you will both enjoy simultaneous pleasure.

If you do not have a headboard, try this variation. As he penetrates her, she raises her arms over her head, pressing her palms flat against a wall. The wall "braces" her body which means that all his thrusts will be felt more intensely by both lovers. To ramp up the sensations even more, he can push some pillows under her buttocks.

It's raunchy because ...
you both feel the urgency of each other's desire. You let go of all your inhibitions and move wildly so your bodies slam into each other on every thrust. You expend all your sexual tension, so afterward you feel completely weak and satiated.

Holding him tight
pleasuring from the inside

There is an intensely satisfying technique that women can use on men: it involves squeezing and rippling the vaginal muscles around his penis. The man has the fantastic experience of being hugged internally. Sheikh Nefzawi calls this a woman's "sucking power" and says it is a prime source of pleasure during sex for many men.

Well-known secret *The Perfumed Garden* is not the only erotic text to sing the praises of "sucking power." The *Ananga Ranga* also recommends that a woman "must ever strive to close and constrict the *yoni* until it holds the *lingam*". Kalyana Malla compares the constrictions of the vagina to "the hand that milks the cow."

Muscle power It is easy to strengthen your vaginal muscles by practicing "Kegel" exercises every day. Your lover will benefit and so will you, since women with toned vaginal muscles have stronger orgasms and more intense sexual sensations.

Start by locating the muscles: you can do this by trying to stop the flow of urine as you pee, or, the sexier option, trying to squeeze your lover's fingers as he caresses you internally. Having identified the correct muscles, find a comfortable position (sitting, lying down, or standing) and slowly contract your muscles as much as possible. Count the number of seconds you can hold the contraction for. Repeat this contraction five more times, and repeat the whole exercise several times a day. Build up to holding the contraction for at least 10 seconds at a time. As well as slow contractions, build in some fast pumping movements to your muscle workout: sharply pull up your muscles and sharply release them—repeat this quickly 10 times, and do it whenever you do the slow contractions.

A thrilling repertoire It may take a few weeks of contractions and pumps before your muscles reach their full strength, but you can start using muscle squeezes during sex right away. Build up a tanatalizing sequence of techniques. Keep your vagina relaxed as he

Secret
make him gasp

After a few weeks of doing Kegel exercises, your muscles should be strong, giving you the "sucking power" Sheikh Nefzawi wrote about. Show off your new skills by giving your lover a special treat.

Save your strongest contraction for the moments immediately before he ejaculates. Wait until you sense he has reached the point of no return, then suddenly contract your muscles as strongly as possible and stay still as he moves inside you. The sudden increase in pressure will make him feel tightly gripped and enhance the intensity of his orgasm.

Try to hold the tight squeeze all the way through his ejaculation and only relax your muscles when he is lying spent and extremely satisfied in your arms.

squeeze to please

enters you, then tell him not to move while you treat him to an incredibly stimulating series of strong, rapid squeezes. Or ripple your muscles against him in gentle pulsating movements. If his erection is flagging, choose a sex position in which your legs are together (to enhance the "tight" sensation) and move on and off him with your muscles contracted as tight as possible—he will find it amazingly reviving.

❝The vagina clings to the member and sucks out the semen by an irresistible attraction ... the member is tightly held until it is drained.**❞**

THE PERFUMED GARDEN

Climaxing together
the secrets of **simultaneous orgasm**

Reaching orgasm at the same time as your lover is both erotically intense and emotionally satisfying, bringing true sexual harmony to your lovemaking. It is held in very high esteem by Sheikh Nefzawi in *The Perfumed Garden*, who urges couples to: "try by all means to make the ejaculations simultaneous because that is the secret of love."

Synchronized passion The contemporary wisdom about simultaneous orgasms is that they are enjoyable only if they are relatively easy to come by. If trying to climax at the same time makes sex frustrating and difficult, concentrate instead on all the other pleasurable aspects of lovemaking. If, however, you are inspired by the erotic challenge of trying to orgasm simultaneously, try synchronizing your sexual responses so that you are both equally aroused throughout sex. So if he is red hot with desire while she is just warm, she will need lots of sexual attention (for example, her favorite orgasmic position, or some top-up stimulation by hand) and he will need to calm down by moving at a slower speed, or by focusing his attentions on her for a while.

Become a voyeur If you are the less aroused partner, exploit your lover's enjoyment—use it to get turned on yourself. Listen to your lover's sexy moans, watch the gorgeous way the body writhes, jerks, or undulates, and the facial expressions of ecstasy. Fetishize every part of your lover's body and feast your eyes upon him or her.

Vary your position An excellent position that targets the hotspots of both partners at the same time is a man-on-top position in which he slides further up her body than usual (aim for his lips to be opposite her forehead). This pushes the base of his shaft tightly against her clitoris on each thrust. Now she rocks her pelvis upward on each of his inward strokes and rocks it backward on each of his outward strokes. This produces a delicious grinding and rubbing pressure that should take you both to orgasm.

Secret
learn to hover

In homage to the Sheikh's belief that sexual fulfillment is the result of prolonged lovemaking, next time you masturbate each other, get to the point where you are about to reach orgasm, then ask your partner to stop. Let your arousal level decrease slightly and then repeat this technique a couple more times. This will teach both of you what it is like to be hovering on the brink of orgasm, but not quite tipping over the edge.

If you can get into this hovering state when you are making love, it is much easier to climax at exactly the same moment as your lover.

Like many of the Tantric techniques this one can take time to master, but with practice you will both soon have much more control over when you climax (see p74).

the art of **perfect timing**

Other techniques Instead of having a simultaneous orgasm during intercourse, try having one during mutual oral or manual sex. When you are stimulating each other by hand or by mouth, it is easier to adjust the speed and pressure, or scale the intensity up or down depending on what your lover needs. Or try a mix-and-match approach; for example, she can masturbate while she gives him oral sex. Or you can both masturbate while lying beside each other—this makes it easier to pace yourselves, and what you lose in intimacy, you can make up for with lots of kissing and eye contact. Plus, watching each other masturbate can be incredibly enlightening because you learn what really pleasures your partner by witnessing the techniques he or she uses.

❝Kisses, nibbles, sucking of lips, close clasping of breasts … these are the things that ensure durable affection and make the two ejaculations occur simultaneously.**❞**

THE PERFUMED GARDEN

Coitus from the Back

She drapes herself seductively across a mound of cushions or pillows that push her bottom up slightly. **FOR HIM** As the passion mounts, she raises her bottom higher—this looks amazingly sexy and should tempt him to lavish her buttocks with kisses and caresses before he enters her. In fact, he can give her oral sex before getting into the position. Once he is inside her, his position enables him to thrust passionately. **FOR HER** She will swoon with G-spot (see p36) pleasure because the angle at which he enters her means that the tip of his penis should firmly press on this peak erogenous zone. Unlike other rear-entry positions, she does not need to support herself on her hands and knees, so she is free to relax, close her eyes, and give herself over to the incredible erotic bliss.

To change the mood and tempo, he can take a break from thrusting, rest quietly inside her, and lean forward to kiss her.

It's passionate because …

she can sense his lust from his deep and fast thrusts. This inspires her to moan and push her bottom up even higher to meet him. Both partners feed off the intensity until it pushes you both gloriously over the edge.

Gripping with Toes

This unusual sex position involves her wrapping her legs around him and crossing her ankles behind his back. She is partly suspended from his body, which feels thrilling for both lovers.

Try this passionate sequence for getting into the Gripping with Toes position: start in Suspended Congress (see p46), in which he picks her up in a standing position and she wraps her legs around his waist. Then he carries her to the bed and lowers her body.

FOR BOTH She rests her upper back, shoulders, and head on the bed but leaves her legs clasped around his waist. He abandons himself to her movements that drive both lovers crazy.

It's passionate because ...

her tightly clasped legs show him just how much she wants him. She can also use her thigh muscles to pull herself up and down on his body. And when he can no longer resist not moving, he can put his hand under her hips, draw her up, and thrust deeply.

"We were having sex standing up. **He suddenly picked me up and carried me to bed**, and we finished making love as I took control by wrapping my legs around his waist.**"**

Love's Tailor

and other **explosive sex moves**

The way in which you and your lover move during sex can yield some sizzling sensations for both of you. Your moves can also change the mood of lovemaking from sensual to feverish in an instant. In *The Perfumed Garden*, Sheikh Nefzawi recommends a variety of movements, described below, to help you get maximum pleasure.

Love's Tailor To set the mood for rampant sex, he should try this teasing opener. He inserts the tip of his penis inside her and makes tiny back and forth rubbing movements. The friction will feel fantastic on the acutely sensitive area just inside her vagina. Then, just when she is relaxing into these blissful sensations, he gives her an erotic jolt by suddenly sliding all the way in.

Bucket in the Well Embrace each other closely in a face-to-face sex position and then take turns to move alternately: he thrusts in and out, then she thrusts, and so on. Increase the pace as you go and do not worry if, by the moment of climax, sex is so wild that you have abandoned the careful discipline of taking turns.

The Mutual Shock This is a move that will make you gasp as your bodies slam together on each stroke. After penetration, pull yourselves apart so that just the tip of the penis remains inside. Pause for a tantalizing moment and then push forward quickly so your bodies collide and the penis enters deeply once more. Now repeat this technique, but make sure you are extremely well lubricated.

Love's Bond She lies still while he penetrates her deeply and then grinds with his pelvis without removing even the smallest portion of his penis from her vagina. *The Perfumed Garden* is passionate about the benefits of this simple movement: women love it because it gives both deep vaginal and clitoral stimulation. Sheikh Nefzawi says it "procures them the greatest pleasure." A man benefits from being deeply and snugly enclosed, and the unusual plane of movement means that he can last longer.

Secret

taking turns

The moves that arouse him the most may be different from those that work for her, and vice versa. For example, he might love in-out thrusting, whereas she prefers keeping all of him inside her as she grinds against him. Sheikh Nefzawi has a simple problem-solving secret: he called it "going shares." This is a great way for both of you to receive the targeted pleasure you need, without either of you feeling selfishly dominant.

She sits astride his body, facing away from him, and grinds against him until she is breathless. Then she stops and gets into a kneeling or squatting position, which is his cue to get up and start thrusting. Continue alternating in this way until she reaches orgasm; then he is free to thrust his way to a climax.

targeting the **hotspot**

"Prepare her for the enjoyment and let nothing be neglected to attain this end. Explore her with all possible activity ..."

THE PERFUMED GARDEN

Enhancing orgasm
taking pleasure to the **highest level**

After the foreplay and intercourse comes the supreme moment of sex: orgasm. To enjoy what *The Perfumed Garden* calls a "delightful copulation that leaves a delicious memory," try the techniques below to find what works best for both of you. The aim is to maximize sensations so that both partners experience a truly memorable orgasm.

Secret

x-rated thoughts

For an intense orgasm, stimulate your mind as well as your body. Choose a position, such as Fitting on of the Sock (see p118), that gives you an incredibly titillating view of your lover's body or genitals. Being able to see each other's genitals in close-up will charge your erotic imagination and trigger some x-rated thoughts. Share those thoughts aloud as you make love. Thrill your lover with an erotic narrative in which you describe what you are doing and how amazing it feels. On another occasion, experiment by doing the opposite: close your eyes and give in to a very naughty and private fantasy. Your lover need never know what is fueling your excitement!

The perfect fit The best orgasms happen when you choose a position that perfectly suits you and your lover—perhaps because you both find it intensely arousing or because of the way your bodies fit together. For example, if she has a sensitive G-spot and he enjoys freedom to thrust, a rear-entry position will be mutually blissful. Or if she likes firm clitoral pressure and he enjoys being on his back, a woman-on-top position could give both lovers satisfying orgasms. Simple man-on-top positions may also be orgasmic because his pubic bone neatly presses against her clitoris. So study the way your hotspots join together and choose what works best for you. As Sheikh Nefzawi says: "It is advisable that the connoisseur of copulation should try all the postures so that he may know which gives them most pleasure."

Scintillating sensations As well as choosing the best position, maximize sensation by caressing each other with your hands during sex. He can give her intense orgasms by stroking her clitoris, especially when she is sitting astride him face on. Caressing or tweaking her nipples when she is near orgasm can also magnify her excitement. In return, she can take him to the height of ecstasy by using her fingertips to lightly caress his testicles, or stroke or penetrate his anus—this will fire up all his pleasure spots leading to a sensation overload and a powerful orgasm.

Find out if your lover has any favorite ways of being touched. Alternatively, just experiment by sucking his or her fingers or toes during sex, and nibbling, scratching, or spanking (see p21 and p62).

Rainbow Arch

This position is also known as Drawing the Bow, which describes the sexy way her body is pulled tautly against his. To get into this position, he slides between her legs as she lies on her side. He lies behind her, braces himself by placing a hand on her shoulder and enters her. She leans forward so she can grasp his leg. Now that both have made a stable frame with their bodies, they simply hold on and enjoy the ride. **FOR HIM** The gorgeous curves of her buttocks and back will inspire him to move with abandon. **FOR HER** She can surrender herself to the intense G-spot stimulation this position provides.

It's ravishing because ...
it feels free, wild, and naughty. In particular, you both have an exhilarating sense of anonymity, which means you can enjoy a secret fantasy. No one is watching, so you can allow your imagination to run free.

❝I was surprised by how much she enjoyed sex in the Rainbow Arch position. She told me afterward that she'd never experienced such **intense physical sensations** during sex.**❞**

Second Posture

This is a maximum impact position for moments of peak lust.
FOR HER Because the woman's legs are raised over her head,
her vagina is contracted, which means she will feel incredibly full.
This is why *The Perfumed Garden* recommends the Second Posture
for men who aren't well endowed: "If your member is short, lay
her on her back and raise her legs so that her toes touch her ears."
This does not mean that a man with a large penis should avoid
this position. **FOR BOTH** As long as he uses a shallow thrusting
technique, both partners can experience fantastic sensations.

It's ravishing because ...

it is high impact and high intensity
and you can communicate with
each other through sexy eye contact
(which will make him aware of exactly
what moves she likes and how to
adjust the depth of his thrusts). You
can both witness each other's every
shudder of ecstasy.

Do it differently
shake up your **sex life**

Keeping things naughty and varied is the secret to maintaining an exciting and fulfilling sex life. *The Perfumed Garden* tells lovers to be inventive in their pleasure-seeking. Try giving your lover the thrill of the unexpected tonight—do something that will make your lover glow with pleasure, and leave him or her with a wonderful memory.

Naughty venues Give your lover a long kiss, then lead him or her to the kitchen. Press your lover against the fridge, continue kissing, and begin taking off your lover's clothes. Drizzle the naked skin with something sexy from the kitchen, such as cream or honey and begin licking it off (see p112). Men: when she is aroused, lift her onto the kitchen counter and let passion take its course.

Your new and naughty erotic venue needn't be the kitchen at all. It could also be the rug in front of the fireplace, the private swimming pool on vacation, behind a tree or a bush in your backyard, in front of the bathroom mirror, on the dining room table, or on any other piece of furniture. Making love in a new place often means an exciting new position—standing, leaning, bending over, or even hanging from a bar or branch, rather than lying in bed.

Personalized positions If you cannot find enough sex positions to satisfy you, Sheikh Nefzawi simply advises that you make up your own. Try doing this tonight (and give your invention its own special name). If one or both of you do yoga or gymnastics, try adapting your favorite pose into a sex position.

Enjoy a sex soiree Have a party for two. Smooch to your favorite sexy music. Seduce each other over a glass of champagne, and present your lover with an erotic gift that pushes back the sexual boundaries—for example, a pair of ankle cuffs, an erotic DVD, a skin-tight rubber top, some silk restraints, or a toy to stimulate her G-spot or his P-spot (see p158). Suggest with a mischievous smile that your lover should wear, watch, or use the gift right now.

Secret
erotic appointment

According to the Sheikh, the King used to arrange a time to consort with his lover and wait under the bedouin tent for her to appear. Why not behave like royalty for a night and make a "sex appointment" with your lover?

Arrange a time in advance so that you both have the chance to build up an erotic appetite. At the agreed time, greet your lover in bed, dressed for the special occasion.

Women: make sure you wear something stunning that you've never worn before: a burlesque-style corset; fishnet gloves and stockings; stilettos and a feather boa, or a fantasy costume (French maid, for example)—a costume you know will ensure his undivided attention all night.

> "... if anyone should think the number (of positions) given is too small, he has nothing to do but invent some more." **THE PERFUMED GARDEN**

Sizzling pleasures
from
China

"The mutual fulfillment of man and woman is like the mutual dependence of heaven and earth." *THE CLASSIC OF SU NU*

Sizzling pleasures from China
the world of *The Tao*

The ancient Taoists have a lot to teach modern lovers about sex. Whereas we might see orgasm as the grand pinnacle of sexual pleasure, the Taoists believed exactly the opposite. Men were advised to refrain from ejaculation so that they could enjoy not just greater and longer-lasting pleasure with their partner, but good health, too.

History Taoism is an ancient Chinese philosophy that advocates living in harmony with nature. The most famous Taoist erotic text is *The Classic of Su Nu*, dates back to the 1st century. It takes the form of a Q&A session between the Yellow Emperor and Su Nu (his female advisor on all things erotic).

Common problems The questions the Yellow Emperor asks are surprisingly similar to questions men might ask today: What if I can't get an erection? What if my partner does not get aroused? How can I tell if she is enjoying sex? Yet, Su Nu's answers are more lyrical than those of contemporary sex experts. She advises him to follow his desires, reassuring him that a woman's body "naturally undulates upward to meet the man's." She encourages him to throw himself into the glorious union of female energy *Yin* and male energy *Yang*. It is through the sexual union of *Yin* and *Yang*, she says, that men and women become whole, happy, and enjoy a long and healthy life as a loving couple.

Holding back Su Nu cautioned the Emperor against ejaculating: "When *Ching* (semen) is emitted the whole body feels weary." She claimed that

exercising self-control and "calming the passion" would allow more love to grow between lovers. This advice does not mean that men may never ejaculate, but that they should make their ejaculations infrequent to preserve their *yang*.

Understandably, many modern men would not want to forgo the pleasure and release of ejaculation, of course. Fortunately, there is another way to take advantage of Taoist teachings: to do specific sex exercises (see p144), and use the passion-extending techniques to gain greater control during sex, so that men can enjoy the bliss of a long lovemaking session (or several) and then ejaculate when the moment's right for both partners.

A woman's pleasure The emphasis on prolonging sex has obvious benefits for women, too. She can languish in sensuality and take all the time she needs to reach orgasm, rather than feeling pressured to climax. Plus, from a Taoist point of view, she has time to bask in all his nourishing *yang* energy and feel a fantastic sense of peace and well-being after making love. Perhaps, then, it is no surprise that some of the most influential Taoist sexologists, such as Su Nu, have been women.

"In our universe all lives are created through the **harmony of Yin and Yang.** When Yang has the harmony of Yin, all his problems will be solved, and when Yin has the harmony of Yang, all obstacles on her way will vanish. One Yin and one Yang must constantly assist one another." *THE CLASSIC OF SU NU*

Sex exercises for her
enhance **sexual pleasure**

According to Chinese erotic texts, sex exercises are a wonderful way for a woman to increase her sexual vitality and satisfaction. The techniques outlined below—massaging the breasts daily or wearing jade balls prior to lovemaking—can provide the opportunity for some erotically rich self-indulgence, and make a woman more sexually aware when she is intimate with her lover.

The deer exercise This is a simple and popular Chinese exercise that is designed to spread sexual pleasure and *yin* energy throughout a woman's body and increase the chances of a clitoral, vaginal, or even whole-body orgasm.

Start by sitting naked on the floor, with your heel pressed against your clitoris and vagina—enjoy the pleasure of its touch. Rub your palms together to warm them, then move them in slow circles on your breasts. Make your hands lightly brush the skin of your breasts and nipples but don't move your breasts. Close your eyes and tune in to the erotic feelings centered in your nipples. Then, after you have completed 36 circles, let your hands rest in your lap and contract your vaginal muscles once. Hold the contraction for as long as possible and let sensual feelings spread throughout your body.

Toned and tight To gain maximum pleasure from sex, the Chinese—and other Eastern teachings—believe a woman should have strong and powerful vaginal muscles. The traditional way to achieve this was for the woman to insert one or two jade balls inside her vagina. As she went about her daily activities, she naturally contracted her muscles to keep the balls inside her—over time, the result was a lithe and toned vagina. (See also pages 120–121.)

Or, wear *ben wa* balls (see opposite) for an hour before making love (these can be purchased from sex boutiques), or slide a vibrator in your vagina, clenching your muscles to keep it inside you. This vaginal workout raises awareness of your internal erogenous zones, which teaches you how to experience peak pleasure during sex.

Secret
sexy hip circles

Do you want to be worshipped by your lover for giving him amazing sensations when you are on top during sex? Prepare yourself with the following exercise when you are alone: stand with your legs apart and bend your knees slightly. Contract your vaginal muscles and very slowly move your hips in circles 10 times one way and 10 times the other. Keep the upper part of your body still, and make your hip swirls sensual and voluptuous. Do a number of sets. Memorize the movement as you do it.

Next time you are on top of your lover during sex, contract your muscles and begin simulating the sexy hip circles. He will feel that you have truly taken charge and benefit from some wonderful sensations as you contract your vaginal muscles.

"Swallows in Love is my favorite position. **I adore the feeling of his weight on top of me ...** it's just the sensation of being covered and consumed by him."

Swallows in Love

This is the position you are likely to adopt when you want to be affectionate with each other. No other position quite matches it for simplicity, closeness, and face-to-face intimacy. Even though the man is on top, she can help control his pace and rhythm by prompting him while holding his waist or his buttocks.

FOR BOTH Try whispering to each other as you make love in this position. Take advantage of the emotional intimacy to express your most tender feelings. Punctuate your words with long kisses. You will notice how the combination of talking and kissing propels you to new levels of love, intimacy, and lust.

It's sensual because ...
you can both relax your bodies and enjoy the erotic sensations radiating out from your genitals. You can also relish the subtle sensations of sex: her fingers running down his back, his breath against her cheek, her thighs pressing against him, and the weight of his chest pressing against her soft breasts.

Mandarin Duck

He enters her from behind in the spoons position, then she twists so she's half lying on her back. This means he can raise himself on one elbow and lean over her body to kiss her face, neck, or breast. This is a gentle rear-entry position that is perfect for a loving start to the day or an erotic end to the evening. Although there is no direct friction on her clitoris, his penis should directly stimulate her G-spot and he can easily reach her breasts to tweak and caress her nipples. **FOR HER** She can vary the sensations both partners experience by pulling one or both knees up close to her chest.

FOR BOTH After sex, lie together and savor the intimacy. Enjoy the post-orgasmic high by stroking and petting each other gently. This is a heavenly position in which to drift off to sleep.

It's sensual because ... the bodies fit together perfectly and she loves the warmth and comfort of his naked body wrapped around hers. It is easy to get into a gorgeous groove of movement by gently rocking against each other.

"We often **make love** in this position in the morning because it's a natural progression from spooning. It's wonderfully **emotional and tender.**"

Cicada on a Bough

This rear-entry position is perfect for blissfully deep penetration. He should take care to enter her slowly, teasing her with shallow strokes at first, then gradually enter more deeply so she has a chance to reach a peak point of arousal (the more aroused she is, the deeper he can go because her uterus lifts up, making more space at the top of her vagina). **FOR BOTH** Enjoy the fact that you can share sweet cheek-to-cheek intimacy in Cicada on a Bough. Although mouth-to-mouth kissing can be a bit awkward, the male lover can whisper sweet nothings to his partner, nuzzle her ear, and gently kiss or stroke her face.

Her body is covered by his, but she can still play an active role by wiggling or jerking her hips. **FOR HER** If she wants to achieve the tightest fit possible, she can close her legs and squeeze him tightly with her vaginal muscles.

It's sensual because ...

on each inward thrust, the tip of his penis nudges, strokes, and caresses her G-spot. The more stimulation the G-spot gets, the more sensitive and responsive it becomes. If she angles her bottom up high (placing pillows under her hips helps), the sensations increase. His slow, gliding strokes will lead her to a state of intense bliss.

Humming Bird

This is a perfect beginning and end to a short sequence of woman-on-top positions. She starts in Humming Bird with her arms around him as both partners delight in the feeling of his penis fully enclosed in her vagina. Then, when she wants to move more freely, she kneels in an upright position and grinds or thrusts against him.

FOR HER She should find exactly the position and angle that aligns her clitoris with his pubic bone, then move against it—the friction will help her to reach a lovely wave of bliss, if not orgasm.

FOR HIM She can help him to climax by kneeling up so her buttocks lift off his body and his penis slides a little way out of her vagina. This gives him room to thrust his hips from underneath. Finally, for the post-orgasmic come-down, she can lean forward for a gorgeous and loving embrace.

It's sensual because ...

it is as much a full-body cuddle as a sex position. She can rest her head on his chest or shoulder while he puts his arms around her and strokes her back. Meanwhile she cradles his shoulders and presses him intimately with her thighs. The soft weight of her body and the warm crush of her breasts are pure delight.

Sex exercises for him
enhance sexual pleasure

Chinese erotic texts, such as *Secrets of the Jade Chamber* (written over 2,000 years ago), suggest that men should do daily exercises designed to increase their sexual prowess and give them new sexual sensations in addition to orgasm. These techniques include the "deer"—a way of cultivating sexual energy—and exercises specifically developed to make a man's penis strong and powerful.

Deer exercise He should try doing this traditional Chinese exercise as an alternative to masturbating. Instead of the quick pleasure of ejaculation, it spreads a tingling feeling throughout his body. It also enhances his sexual vitality, and increases his enjoyment and chance of having a whole-body orgasm during sex.

Do the deer exercise naked while sitting or lying in a warm, comfortable room. To begin with, rub your hands together and place them over your penis for a minute to get into a relaxed state. Then cup your testicles with your right hand and rest the thumb on the base of your penis. Close your eyes and savor the gentle warmth and pressure from your hand to your genitals. Put your left hand on your pubic area, just below your belly button, and rub your hand in 81 clockwise circles, concentrating on the warm, sensual feelings building up beneath your hand. Now swap the position of your hands and use your right hand to rub your pubic area in 81 counterclockwise circles. Feel the warmth growing and spreading. Finally, rest your hands on your lap and contract the muscles of your perineum (between your scrotum and anus). Hold the contraction for as long as it feels comfortable and enjoy the glorious feeling of the tingling energy which will gradually move up your body.

Jade stalk strengthening In China, it was traditional for a man to do a penile version of weightlifting by tying two small weights to either end of a small length of soft rope and then draping it over the base of his erect "jade stalk" (penis). Then he would lift the weights 20 to 50 times each day to strengthen his penile muscles.

Secret
flex your jade stalk

If your lover has ever given you a peak moment of pleasure by contracting her internal muscles around you during your lovemaking (see p120), now is your chance to return the compliment.

Thrill your lover by doing your "jade stalk" lifts while you are inside her. These subtle, movements will give her wonderful sensations, and mark you out as a truly remarkable lover. Try doing 30 intense contractions just after penetration. Ask her to stay still and, to give her maximum pleasure, position the head of your penis against her G-spot so that she can feel you pulsating against this very sensitive area. Now penetrate her very deeply and do some more contractions.

Another penis-strengthening exercise in China was to thrust the penis repeatedly into a bowl of sand, starting with 20 plunges and working up to 100. This is modeled on an exercise called "Iron Hands," in which Shao Lin monks plunged their hands into warm sand to make them strong enough to chop wood and brick.

Today, simple "penis lifts," or Kegel exercises, are the contemporary equivalent of rope or sand exercises. Try repeatedly contracting and relaxing the muscles you would use to stop the flow of urine. Do a combination of intense and moderately intense contractions, aiming for a total of 40 to 60 per day.

"If the man and woman are sympathetic to each other their harmony itself could often make short and small instruments become longer and bigger, and soft and weak ones become harder and stronger.**"**

SECRETS OF THE JADE CHAMBER

Horse Shakes Feet

In this playful position, she lies with one leg stretched across the front of his body, resting it on his shoulder, and has the other leg bent close to her body. **FOR HER** Although he is in a dominant kneeling posture, she can hold him teasingly at bay with her foot on his chest. This allows you both to enjoy the erotic power struggle. **FOR HIM** If he enjoys nipple tweaks and caresses, she can try pinching his nipple between her toes (this takes practice). Alternatively, rub oil into his chest before initiating sex—this enables the woman to slide and glide her toes with ease all over his nipple.

It's steamy because ...

her legs are parted, making it easy for him to caress her clitoris as he thrusts. He can also give her intense sensations by stroking her buttock and the back of her exposed thigh. As the sexual tension mounts, she can brace herself against him by grasping his thighs.

"He was so turned on each time I tweaked his nipple between my toes that **it made him thrust more vigorously**. Strangely, it felt as if I was in control, which was hugely arousing for me.**"**

Phoenix Playing in a Red Cave

The phoenix is a revered creature in China (second only to the dragon) and symbolizes femininity. Rather than using this as a position for hard and fast thrusting, you should both enjoy its elegance and make your movements slow and considered.

FOR HIM He can feast on the sight of her body as he makes love to her and focus on small but acute sensations, such as the bump of his testicles against her buttocks as he moves in and out.

FOR HER To heighten her pleasure, he can try the Nine Shallow, One Deep sequence of thrusting (see p154), but make the deep stroke shallower than usual. For example, he should penetrate only as far as the "valley's proper" (this is the name Taoists give to a spot a few inches into the vagina) so that not all of his penis is inside her.

It's steamy because ...

she is offering him the ultimate sexual invitation as she raises her legs high in the air so he can enter her. He is faced with an open view of her genitals and experiences an incredibly high level of arousal, which she can see on his face.

Ways to extend passion
make love **all night long**

Many Taoists recommend gloriously prolonged periods of lovemaking so that both lovers have a chance to experience waves of ecstasy before reaching a climax. Ancient Chinese texts even go so far as to say that sex should last for a "thousand loving thrusts." To achieve this sexy feat, men may benefit from learning some Chinese delaying techniques.

Satisfy her As mentioned in the introduction on page 136, traditional Chinese teachings say that men should be sparing with the frequency of their ejaculations. Men who can make love without ejaculating are highly praised for their ability to satisfy women: they can continue to make love all night because they do not have to wait for their erection to return. And, as one Taoist master points out: "a man who does not emit would have no trouble in satisfying ten women in a single evening!"

So whether he would like to avoid ejaculation completely during sex or would just like to last a bit longer, these ancient methods of delaying ejaculation can help him enormously.

Secret

the slow route

If he is reaching orgasm too soon, he can take a break by pulling out of his lover, sliding down her body to kiss her belly, her inner thighs, and her "jade gate" (vagina). She will love the oral attention and he will have the chance to delay his orgasm. There might not be evidence to back the Taoist claim that drinking her "jade fluid" during oral sex is restorative, but it will do wonders for the physical relationship, as she will realize that he is an incredibly considerate lover.

The locking method During sex, he should breathe deeply and steadily to keep his mind and body focused. (It is the opposite of the fast panting he does in the lead-up to orgasm.) If he feels he might lose control, he should focus all his attention on his breath, withdraw his penis by about an inch, and stop moving while he contracts his pelvic floor muscles, as if he were trying to stop the flow of urine. (see p145). He starts thrusting again once he feels his arousal levels have dropped a little. The secret to practicing the locking method is to pick the right moment. If he goes past a critical point, he will not be able to stop himself from ejaculating. As the ancient Chinese masters say: "It is much better to retreat too early than too late."

Chinese squeeze While he is thrusting inside her, he remains aware of how aroused she is from one second to the next. As soon as he feels her excitement taking over, he reaches down and presses a spot on his perineum that is halfway between his anus and testicles. He takes a deep breath at the same time and his excitement drops to a controllable level. Done correctly, this rapid and effective technique does not interrupt lovemaking, and enhances her orgasm.

make it **slow and sensual**

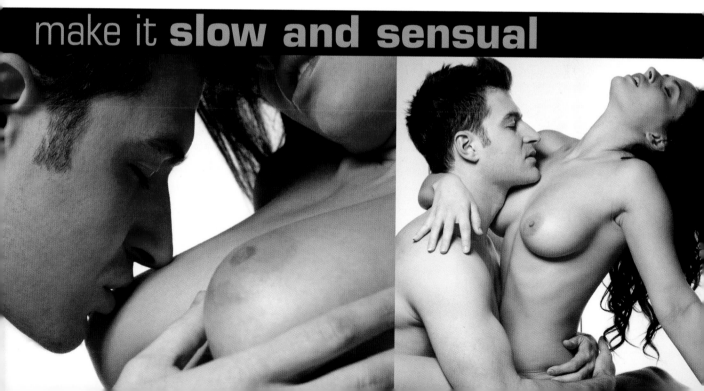

Seagulls on the Wing

She lies back on the bed while he kneels on the floor between her legs. He needs to make sure he is comfortable—he can kneel on a pillow if it helps—then he turns her to putty by swirling his tongue on her clitoris. He then returns to an upright position and follows the advice of the Taoist masters by guiding his penis into her "as slowly as a snake entering a hole to hibernate." **FOR HIM** He should close his eyes and savor the sensations along the shaft of his penis as he slides into her.

FOR HER Seagulls on the Wing is a wonderfully versatile position because she can vary the stance of her legs to create different sensations. If she bends her legs and puts her heels on the edge of the bed, he can enter her more deeply. If she raises her legs and rests her feet on his shoulders, her vagina is foreshortened and every thrust will have greater impact.

It's raunchy because ...

he can look down and see the incredibly thrilling sight of his penis sliding in and out of her vagina. For many men, this kind of visual stimulation can give an instant boost of excitement. Women find this position raunchy because it is very easy to masturbate while experiencing the simultaneous joy of penetrative intercourse.

Birds Fly Back on Back

This is an unusual spin on a woman-on-top position. She straddles him with her back turned to him and controls the pace, movement, and rhythm. **FOR HIM** He enjoys the sexiness of being taken by her. He can take advantage of the fact that her buttocks are close to his hand by cupping them, stroking them, or delivering a light spank when she is least expecting it. **FOR HER** Just as men are instructed by Taoist masters to vary their strokes, so can she. She can lower herself up and down using thigh power, then shake or vibrate her hips, or contract and release her vaginal muscles.

It's raunchy because ...

sex where you cannot see each other's face feels naughty and thrilling—you can each drift off into your own world of private erotic fantasies. And you both have a very sexy view: she can look down to see her vagina enclosing his penis; he can gaze lustfully at her buttocks.

Tiger Step

He kneels behind her while she is on all fours, then she lowers her chest to the bed in this dramatic variation of doggie-style. **FOR HIM** He can use his hands to firmly hold her waist or buttocks or, if she likes having her hair tugged, he can lean forward and take it loosely in his fist. **FOR HER** She can try raising and lowering her chest to discover what different angles feel like. If his movements feel too intense, sliding forward on the bed will put her at a shallower angle and make her feel more comfortable. For a sexy trio of rear-entry positions, start sex on all fours, then move into Tiger Step, then lie flat on your front in Cicada on a Bough (see p142).

It's raunchy because …

she feels deeply submissive and sexy as she raises her buttocks high in the air and rests her cheek on the bed. He is excited by the gorgeous view of her body and the way he can penetrate her freely.

Bamboo

This is one of the most "easy-access" sex positions. It is a simple standing posture, which makes it ideal for spontaneous sex. You do not even have to take off your clothes; she can slip off her panties and he can drop his pants.

Getting maximum enjoyment from this position depends on him being able to penetrate her properly. **FOR HIM** If she needs to be higher for him to enter her comfortably, she can stand on tiptoes, wear heels, or stand on a step. Alternatively, he can squat while she parts her legs and pushes her pelvis toward him for wonderfully deep penetration. If full penetration is a challenge, he should try thrusting between her thighs. **FOR HER** She can be driven wild by his grinding movement which nudges her clitoris and vaginal entrance, then he can thrill her by picking her up and penetrating her. She may choose to wrap her thighs around his waist.

It's raunchy because ... you can graduate from passionate clinch to full-on sex in an instant. And if you were not expecting to have sex, but the mood just swept you away, you can both delight in a sense of wicked, impulsive lust.

"We'd been sending each other sexy text messages from work all day. As soon as I got home **I found her leaning enticingly against the hallway wall** waiting for me. We had brief, explosive sex in Bamboo."

Staying shallow then going in deep
the art of **penetration**

According to the ancient Chinese texts, the secret to giving a woman heightened satisfaction was to thrust at specific depths inside her vagina. There are eight lyrically named "valleys," including Lute String (one inch into the vagina), Black Pearl (four inches), and the North Pole (entire penis). Try using different depths of thrusting to enhance your lovemaking.

Nine Shallow and One Deep Ancient Chinese masters advised men to follow a thrusting pattern of nine shallow strokes followed by one deep stroke throughout sex. This technique, they said, would make women weak with pleasure. He should try penetrating his lover up to her Little Stream (three inches), then thrust nine times, followed by one deeper thrust to her Inner Door (six inches). If he repeats this all the way through sex, he can stay in control until he decides to succumb to a dizzying orgasm. If he needs to last longer, he can use the Chinese techniques of ejaculation control (see p148).

The right thrust for you Although the "Nine Shallow" technique is widely favored by Chinese masters, experiment to find your own thrusting sequence that feels fantastic. Try five shallow and one deep, or three shallow and one deep, for example. And ask your lover what depth of strokes she needs to take her to orgasm. She might prefer only shallow thrusting, which stimulates her G-spot and the internal parts of her clitoris; or only deep thrusting, which stimulates the pleasure spots at the very top of her vagina. If you and your lover have never experimented with different levels of penetration, try devoting a whole sex session to varying depths of thrust and, afterward, have a very intimate conversation about which technique felt best and why.

Secret
bucking, thrusting, and plunging

He can vary his thrusts to find which works best for her. Chinese erotic manuscripts use striking images that help you visualize how to move. For example, try "moving up and down like a wild horse bucking through a stream"; or use deep thrusts and shallow teasing strokes that alternate as "swiftly as a sparrow picking the leftovers of rice in a mortar"; or try "rising then plunging low like a huge sailing boat braving the gale"; or "strike out to the left and right as a brave warrior trying to break up the enemy ranks." If you wish to be gentle, "push in slowly as a snake entering a hole to hibernate."

perfect **thrusts**

Huge Bird Above a Dark Sea

This position is simple, but intensely passionate. Lying on her back, the woman raises her legs, allowing him to lean forward, lift her bottom, and rest it on his thighs. He can then penetrate her deeply by placing his arms around her waist.

FOR BOTH In Chinese terms, this position allows men to express the qualities of strength and movement, and women to express the qualities of stillness and receptiveness. In other words, it is an ideal communion of *yin* and *yang*.

It is easy to get carried away in Huge Bird Above a Dark Sea. He can try a Taoist technique, such as the locking method to control his excitement (see p149). This way, he will be able to continue making love for as long as he wants. **FOR HIM** It is said that a man who has mastered the *Tao* can completely satisfy his lover without fail.

It's passionate because ...

he can swoop down bird-like and enter with a single dramatic thrust. As the erotic text *T'ung Hsuan Tzu* says: "poise, then strike like an eagle." Lovers can also share a lustful gaze at that special moment of penetration.

Cat and Mouse Sharing a Hole

She lies full frontal on his body in a close hug and then pushes herself up into a semi push-up. For an extremely sexy touch, there is the option of holding hands while she does this.

Many men rate this as one of the most erotic woman-on-top positions. **FOR HIM** Not only can he enjoy the closeness of her body, he can also gaze up at her face and feel the glorious sensations of her hair tickling his skin and her nipples grazing his chest. **FOR HER** There is a lot of scope for movement, too: she can bump her pelvis up and down, wiggle from side to side, or move in slow undulating circles. She can also push herself up and down on a horizontal plane by pushing off from his feet.

It's passionate because ...

she can push him back on the bed and climb on top to feed her insatiable lust. And because she is supported on her arms, she is free to make fast frenzied movements that drive both partners to a level of complete rapture.

Finding his G-spot
the ultimate **pleasure point**

Stimulating his G-spot with your fingers can give him an immediate sexual high, leading to a more thrilling orgasm—and a new sensation to the one he usually experiences directly through his penis. The Chinese way of accessing the G-spot is via a special place on the perineum called *Hui Yin*, which means "the gate of life and death."

His pleasure point The male G-spot, also known as the "P-spot," is actually the prostate gland—a small gland that lies inside the body just underneath a man's bladder, which is sensitive to sexual stimulation. Although you cannot touch the prostate directly, there are two indirect ways of stimulating it: through the perineum or via the anus. Exploring his G-spot is easier if you use massage oil or another type of sex lubricant.

Pressing *Hui Yin* This is the most accessible route to giving him G-spot ecstasy. She should slide her fingers up and down his perineum—the area between his testicles and his anus— caressing him while she locates the pleasure point. Once she has found a spot that feels like a slight indentation halfway between his scrotum and anus, she should gently apply pressure to it with the pad of her fingertip (or the second knuckle of her middle finger if she has long nails). This is his *Hui Yin* spot—also known by the Chinese as the "million dollar spot." Try applying deep static or pulsating pressure and ask him which he enjoys most. Don't be afraid of pressing quite deeply—the area you are stimulating lies inside his body rather than just under his skin. Now take the erotic tension to breaking point by adding some passionate oral sex.

Lasting longer Men can use the *Hui Yin* point to delay ejaculation. They simply press it when they feel themselves getting too excited during sex. Rather than sustaining the pressure, they just press it briefly until they feel back in control. This technique is sometimes called the Chinese squeeze (see p149).

Secret
give him peak pleasure

Once you have familiarized yourself with your lover's G-spot, make him convulse with pleasure by stimulating all his hotspots at once: his penis, his testicles, his *Hui Yin* spot, and his anus.

This might sound like a lot of areas to attend to all at once, but you can enlist his help: nestle your face between his legs and invite him to masturbate as you press your finger firmly against his *Hui Yin* point. As he begins to get more aroused, gently flick the tip of your tongue against his testicles and perineum. Now give him maximum pleasure, by using the lubricated tip of your index finger (on your other hand) to stroke, caress, repeatedly tap, or press his anus.

> **"** The true beauty and pleasure of communion are inner feelings. **"**
> *THE CLASSIC OF SU NU*

unique **sensations**

Alternative access If she wants to get really close to his prostate, she can press it through the wall of the rectum. She should first massage his anus with lubricant so that she can glide her finger smoothly inside him. Now she feels gently along the front belly-side wall for a raised area or just somewhere that feels "different" in texture. If she presses and caresses this area while licking or stroking his penis at the same time, the result will be mind-blowing for him, taking him to new peaks of pleasure.

Galloping Horse

Sex can be fast and impetuous in this position. Galloping Horse has a kinky overtone because the man appears to be holding the woman down. In reality, the restraining force is minimal, and more symbolic than real: he lightly clasps the back of her neck with one hand and grips her ankle with the other.

FOR BOTH You can fantasize about being submissive or dominant—as long as it turns you on. In fact, it is an excellent way to discover whether bondage is something you'd like to explore further. If you are able to control your orgasm to the point where you can have a simultaneous orgasm, try it in Galloping Horse.

FOR HER Taoist masters say that if a woman climaxes at the same time as the man, he is releasing *ching* (see p136) into her body, which is said to have a wonderfully rejuvenating effect on her.

It's ravishing because ...

both of you get swept away on a tidal wave of excitement. She is pinned underneath him and can surrender completely to the erotic sensation. He is in charge and enjoys having a free rein to move.

Horse Cross Feet

As she lies back on the bed, he grabs one of her ankles and pushes her leg up so her knee is pressed hard against her breast. This opens her up to him so he can penetrate firmly while she feels securely locked in position. As the passion rises, he can hook her leg over his shoulder and lean in close for a kiss.

FOR HIM He can try this Taoist thrusting technique: jab the "jade peak" (penis) back and forth in short and slow thrusts inside her "jade gate" (vagina), "as if a farmer is preparing his land for late planting." **FOR HER** She can enjoy the sexy feeling of him bearing down on top of her and reach up to caress the contours of his chest with her hands, or push her fingertips into his mouth.

It's ravishing because ...

she feels taken and he feels in charge. The erotic atmosphere gets more intense by the second as he thrusts feverishly and she pulls him deeper inside her.

"When I play a **dominant role** during sex, both of us get incredibly carried away, **abandoned, and excited**. It's phenomenal!**"**

Salacious pleasures
from
Japan

"A woman will gasp with ecstasy when a man's penis touches her greatest depths ..."

ILLUSTRATED MANUAL OF EROTICISM

Salacious pleasures from Japan

the world of **Zen erotica**

Japan has a wonderfully erotic culture dating back thousands of years. Most famously, it has always had some form of pleasure quarter offering erotic entertainment. Moreover, Japanese art and literature have been incredibly open about sex, considering it a part of life to be explored and enjoyed.

Erotic art The Japanese appreciation of sex is evident from the wealth of sex manuals, explicit woodblock prints, sexual paintings, erotic poetry, and sex toys that date back to the 17th century (when the country's erotic culture flourished). If you have ever felt shy about a particular sex act, take comfort from the fact that it probably wouldn't have been a taboo in Japan, and there is perhaps some allusion to it in one or more of its erotic art forms.

History of hedonism The pinnacle of Japanese eroticism and sensuality came in the "Edo period" (1603 to 1868). "Pleasure quarters," or red light districts, sprung up in every town or city, the most famous being Yoshiwara (present-day Tokyo). With its thoroughfare bustling with erotic thrill-seekers, and streets that were constantly illuminated by lanterns, Yoshiwara became known as the "nightless city." The city was frequented by samurai, merchants, artists, and writers, who visited the courtesans for their erotic entertainment. Eventually, Yoshiwara became the country's hotspot where people could abandon themeslves to decadent hedonism.

Geishas It was in this period that the Japanese geisha gained popularity. Technically, geishas were not prostitutes but entertainers, skilled in the arts of calligraphy, dance, poetry, singing, and erudite conversation—but in some circumstances their services did extend to the erotic. For example, when a wealthy man paid extra money for the services of a geisha he took a liking to, she sometimes became his companion—both personal and sexual.

An alluring feature about geishas was their utterly composed and seductive style; their ability to combine poise with flirtatiousness and femininity. Discover how to play the part of a geisha on page 170.

Further delights This chapter also contains gorgeous Japanese sex techniques. For a steamy bedtime treat, slip between the sheets with your lover to explore the raunchy art of *Shunga* (see pp178–179), or enjoy a naughty sex toy session with plenty of *harigata* (dildo) play (see pp174–175). Or, if you prefer your pleasure to be kinky, turn to pages 182–183 and 186 to be inspired by the arts of dominance, submission, and bondage.

❝With hearts all willing the men duly paid the ransom asked to secure the courtesans' release from their contracts. **Each retired with his concubine to a house in Saga** or led a secluded life in the shadows of Higashiyama or dwelt unknown in Fuji-no-Mori.❞ *THE LIFE OF AN AMOROUS MAN*

Erotic meditation
enter the **realm of the senses**

An enticing quality of a Japanese geisha was her Zen-like serenity. (*Zen* in this context meaning complete immersion.) Whether she was reciting poetry, pouring saki, or caressing a lover, she was entirely poised and focused on what she was doing. By bringing this level of attention and awareness to sex, you can experience some intense and deeply fulfilling moments with your lover.

The right ambience To get into a mindful or meditative state with your lover, make sure you are in a quiet and dimly lit environment with minimal distractions. You will then find it easier to enter the realm of the senses and abandon yourself to erotic pleasure. Your sexual interaction will be more spontaneous and instinctive because you will be completely relaxed and without inhibitions.

Blissful breathing To begin, sit naked cross-legged on the floor back to back with your lover. Close your eyes and concentrate fully on your lover's back touching yours—feel the pressure, the warmth, and the lovely support it gives you.

Deepen your breath so that your belly swells freely each time you inhale. Let the sounds and sensations of your breath lull you into a state of peace and relaxation. If it helps, picture your breath as the sea flowing in and out of you. Leave any worries behind as you focus on the ebb and flow of your breath and the warm sensation of your lover's body against yours. This works wonderfully if you breathe in synchrony with your lover. Try it for at least 15 minutes—you will start to feel as if you are merging into a single breathing body.

Touching hands Turn to face your lover; hold out your hands and bring your palms together without touching them. Now try this simple touch meditation. Hover your palms against your lover's (see right) and concentrate exclusively on the proximity of your hands. See if you can feel a sense of warmth emanating from your lover's hands. Bring your palms even closer until they are just a hair's breadth away from your lover's. Aside from warmth, you might feel a tingling,

Secret
erotic postcard

An integral part of Zen meditation is visualization. Fantasizing about something that you find erotic during sex can lead to a more intense and fulfilling orgasm.

Try this fast turn-on trick: create a visual image in your mind that has a dramatic aphrodisiacal effect on you. Think of it as a secret erotic postcard that no one else will ever see—this way you can make your picture as naughty, filthy, or daring as you like. You might choose an image of your lover's face as he or she rapturously goes down on you, or an image of a fantasy lover ravishing you. Whatever you choose, visualize your image in rich detail, and retain a mental postcard of it to be referred to whenever you want your arousal levels to soar.

immersed **in the moment**

prickling, or pulsating sensation—try to amplify the sensations just by concentrating on them. Take your lover's hand in yours—softly interlace your fingers in theirs and bask in the blissful contact. Revel in the sensuality of the touch. Squeeze each other's fingers every so often and then relax and feel the energy flowing between you.

Spread the sensation If you can manage to sensitize your hands using this simple technique, just imagine what you can achieve if you meditate on the sensations in your genitals as the penis hovers at the entrance of the vagina, or if you pause just before a kiss with your breath mingling and your lips almost touching. Try going to bed with your lover and bringing this kind of mindful awareness to every erotic act you engage in.

❝We both adore Dew on Cherry Blossom position because it **brings us very close together**, and the connection we have is better than sex in any other position.❞

Dew on Cherry Blossom

He sits in an upright position and she shapes her body to his, gently maneuvering her bottom back so it fits snuggly against him. Think of this as the sitting-up version of the spoons position—it has an intimate feel because there is plenty of skin-to-skin contact. **FOR HER** His lips are close to her ear so he can whisper sexy words to her, or simply nuzzle and nibble her earlobe, mixing it up with the occasional breath of hot air. **FOR HIM** Although his ability to thrust is limited, she can take the lead with a delightful rocking motion, and he can lend support by slipping his hands under her buttocks.

The L-shaped position of your bodies makes this position ideal for sitting against a wall or the headboard of your bed. For a steamy treat, you could also try it in the bath.

It's sensual because ... he can smooth his palms along her silky thighs and over the gentle curves of her waist before he reaches around to cup her breasts in his hands. She can twist around to share a sweet kiss.

Mountain Peaks

Think of this as the perfect interlude during sex—after being on top, she gently lies down between his legs with his penis still inside her. **FOR HIM** She can keep him hard by flexing her vaginal muscles along his shaft, while keeping herself aroused by stroking her clitoris. **FOR HER** And if he has climaxed while she hasn't, this is a great position in which he can help masturbate her to orgasm.

Use your hands to stroke each other's calves. And if you love having your feet touched, try this variation: rest your feet on your lover's chest instead of on the bed. This way your lover can give you a sublime foot massage using the hands, lips, and tongue.

It's sensual because ...
you can both relax while meditating on the pleasure of being erotically joined. Both of you can take deep belly breaths and let yourselves float off on a private wave of contentment.

❝We made love on the couch. At first she was **gyrating madly on top of me**, then she just laid down between my legs and very slowly moved her hips up and down. **It felt incredible.❞**

Geisha nights
saucy seduction techniques

Japanese geishas and courtesans are renowned for their graceful methods of seduction. Rather than jumping straight into bed, they take a sensual and leisurely approach to lovemaking—the aim is to build arousal bit by bit until both lovers are trembling with desire to have each other.

Decadent bath Start the evening by sharing a traditional Japanese bath. Once you have filled the tub, pour in two glasses of sake (this alcoholic drink is said to draw out toxins and make your skin smooth and beautiful). Immerse yourselves and inhale the distinctive fragrance that lifts off with the steam. Stroke and fondle each other, but don't get too carried away … not just yet.

Soap massage Stand up in the bath and drizzle each other's bodies with liquid soap. Embrace in a standing position and slide your hands all over each other's curves and crevices, working up a frothy lather (let your hands linger on each other's hotspots). If you enjoy this soapy massage, you can emulate the Japanese ancient tradition and continue the slippery foreplay in the bedroom: lie down on a waterproof sheet or mattress and slide, glide, and writhe against each other in foreplay that is gloriously soapy.

Make an entrance Women: after your bath, request that your lover waits for you in bed. Make a true geisha-style entrance—glide into the room looking stunning in a kimono and red lipstick (and nothing else). Carry a plate of bite-sized treats: cherries, grapes, small pieces of rich, dark chocolate, or sushi. Kneel beside your lover (with your kimono artfully arranged to reveal a thigh, shoulder, or breast) and feed each other. Gaze into each other's eyes as you eat.

Now slide into bed together and slowly get more intimate. Caress and stroke each other's bodies and slowly work down to the genitals. And when you do, try this geisha technique: dip a paintbrush in lubricant and using slow, delicate brushstrokes, paint the length of his penis. It is guaranteed to send a ripple of pleasure through him.

Secret
naughty foot massage

Women can try a classic technique used by Japanese courtesans during the Edo period. Make sure your feet are looking gorgeous (paint your toenails with crimson nail polish), then sit between his legs and trap his erect penis between the soles of your feet. Drizzle lots of oil over his glans so it runs down his shaft. Now drive him wild by rubbing your feet up and down on his penis. Vary the strokes, pressure, and speed (and try supporting his shaft on the top of one foot while you move the other in firm circles). Use your big toe to tease the tip of his penis, slide it down to his frenulum, and then back up again. Revel in the eye contact as you do so.

whatever **you desire**

Lotus Blossom

She leans back in a dramatic arch, with her breasts thrust forward and her head thrown back. **FOR HER** All of her pleasure points are stimulated: the tip of his penis penetrates high in her vagina, his shaft presses against her G-spot, and he can use his thumb or fingers to caress her clitoris. She can make him dizzy with pleasure by rapidly shaking her hips, or by doing slow and sensual pelvic thrusts.

If she wants to move into a more relaxing position, she can easily get into Mountain Peaks (see p169) from this position. Alternatively, if she wants an intense orgasm, she can sit upright and grind against his pubic bone. **FOR BOTH** If you are both in the mood for a cuddle, you can lean forward and press your bodies together as you kiss. It's a turn-on to keep him guessing what your next move might be.

It's steamy because ...

he can enjoy watching her body in the throes of ecstasy. And she feels gorgeously sexy and supple as she arches her body back—few other sex positions make her body look so taut and her breasts so shapely and touchable.

The See-saw

A great way to get into this position is to start by giving each other oral sex in a "69" position (see p48) with him on all fours while she's flat on her back, then she draws her knees to her chest and he crawls forward and enters her slowly and carefully. Alternatively, you can coat yourselves in massage oil and simply slide into the position.

FOR BOTH Novel erotic sensations are to be expected! His penis is entering her at an unusual angle. It is pushed against the back wall of her vagina, which is the site of two special hotspots. One is high up near the cervix (called the cul-de-sac); the other is opposite the G-spot (called the "PS" spot). He should make his thrusts long, slow, and smooth, and then up the tempo as her moans of joy intensify.

It's steamy because ...
you are trying something deliciously challenging and experimental—just to get into position requires you to engage in some very sexy teamwork. And because you can't see each other's faces, you must communicate in breathless whispers to express how good it feels.

❝We were in a **frisky mood** one night and decided to have sex in this adventurous position. **The sensations surprised us.**❞

Traditional love toys
the joys of *harigata*

Japanese erotica has always had a gloriously liberated attitude toward the use of sex toys. A wide range of dildos, love balls, erection aids, and masturbation devices has appeared in erotic texts and paintings throughout the centuries. Many are available to buy in sex boutiques today.

Harigata The Japanese word for dildo is *harigata*. Dildos were not just functional objects, but artistic creations carved out of wood or fashioned from buffalo horn or tortoiseshell, and often used as part of a woman's sexual initiation. In *Secret Techniques*—a 17th-century Japanese love manual—it is recommended that women should use dildos as a means of discovering pleasure. And two women could expand and enhance their erotic experience by making love together using a double-headed dildo. This was said to lead to a powerful orgasm that would make the heart shake, the whole body go numb, and the vagina "contract strongly against the dildo."

Women: let yourself be inspired by the Japanese lack of inhibition when it comes to seeking sexual fulfillment. Instead of using a sex toy for solitary pleasure, be brazen and invite your lover to watch while you pleasure yourself with a dildo or a vibrator. Let him witness you writhe and moan, then just before you head toward orgasm, breathlessly invite him to make love to you.

Sexy shopping Part of the thrill of sex toys is browsing through the selection and imagining the fun you can have with them. In previous centuries, Japanese women eager for sexual satisfaction would buy sex toys from street peddlers, who would carry wares ranging from hairpins and combs to dildos. For the contemporary equivalent, invite your lover to spend an evening shopping online. Browse traditional Asian sex toys such as *ben wa* balls, for example. Or, search for beautifully crafted dildos, vibrators, anal plugs, and beads. Tell your lover which you find most exciting, and why. And make two purchases—something sexy for him and something sexy for her.

Secret

gorgeous geisha

Women: immerse yourself in the Japanese spirit and be his geisha for the night. Take charge and enjoy playing the refined sex goddess. Ask him to lie back on a bank of soft pillows as you enclose his penis in your mouth. Use your lips and tongue to give him a semi-erection, then surprise him by slipping a penis ring down the length of his shaft so that it fits neatly around the base of his penis. Now massage him to full erection and take advantage by sensually sliding on top.

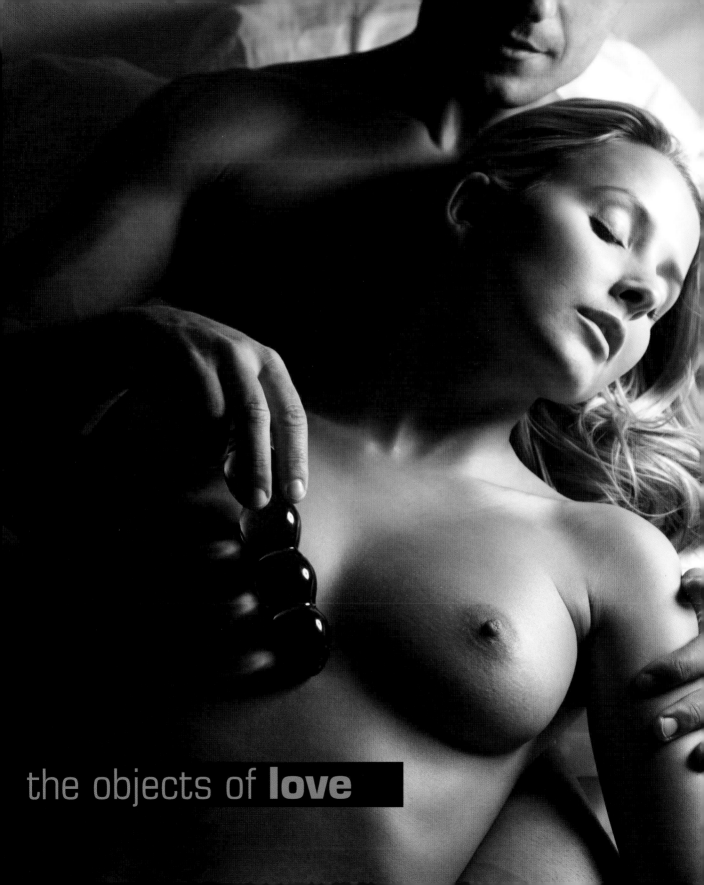

the objects of **love**

The Courtesan

The Courtesan is the ultimate easy-access position for him: all he needs to do is take hold of her hips and enter. **FOR HIM** This, together with the fabulous view of her body stretched out before him, makes the Courtesan a favorite among a lot of men.

FOR HER The rewards are great for her too: despite the steep angle of her body, this is a relaxed, comfortable position for her to savor the feeling of being deeply filled. Her clitoris is within easy reach of her, too. Like most upright positions this works best when his penis is exactly opposite her vagina. It is easy to make height adjustments: he can lower himself by kneeling down or standing with his feet wider apart; she can raise herself with pillows wedged under her buttocks. And if the bed happens to be a futon, he can simply kneel and slip cushions under his knees if the floor is hard.

It's raunchy because ...
she is offering him her body with complete abandonment, and he can look down and revel in the immense turn on of his penis sliding slowly in and out of her. Meanwhile, she can stimulate herself and look forward to a vaginal and clitoral orgasm.

"The Courtesan is the position of choice when I want to **explore my sexiest fantasies**. My body feels incredibly relaxed, as I lie there **visualizing the naughtiest things."**

Swirling Snow

Swirling Snow is easy to get into: sex starts in the spoons position (both partners lie curled up against each other on their sides and he enters from behind), then she pulls away slightly and twists so that she is lying on her back. She then drapes her uppermost leg over his waist or, for a sexy touch, stretches it straight up in the air.

FOR BOTH This sensual position feels fantastic for both: he appreciates the laid-back freedom to thrust while on his side, caressing her body at the same time, and she enjoys the sexy angle of entry and the way his thigh nudges her clitoris on each thrust.

FOR HER When she is close to orgasm, he should stay pressed tight against her body (see p44) and move in a grinding motion rather than thrusting, so that he maintains the exciting clitoral friction, or he can use his hand to take her over the edge.

It's raunchy because ...

it feels laid-back, yet excitingly experimental. It is perfect for a prolonged sex session when lovers can't get enough of each other. She feels penetrated to the fullest, and he can impress her with a range of extremely stimulating moves by merely shifting the angle of entry.

Japanese erotic art
looking at *Shunga*

Japanese erotic art provides lovers with a rich and sensuous source of titillation. The graphic depictions of sex give a fascinating glimpse into Japanese erotic fantasies. If you are in the mood for an unusual type of turn-on, try looking at some *Shunga* pictures with your lover tonight.

History The word *Shunga* means "picture of spring" ("spring" being a euphemism for "sex") and refers to paintings and woodblock prints that were common in Japan between the 17th and 20th centuries. The subject matter is both erotic and explicit, partly because during this period there were twice the number of men compared with women living in the city, and many of them had to rely on erotic art and literature for their sexual gratification.

Larger than life *Shunga* prints include genital close-ups, threesomes, improbable sex positions, and unusual sexual fantasies (the most outlandish being a woman receiving oral sex from an octopus). Men can frequently be seen clutching their gargantuan penises or pushing a towering erection inside a lover. Throughout the Edo period, *Shunga* art explored sex in the most fantastical form possible, and it was appreciated by men and women. In fact, lovers often gave each other *Shunga* prints, and women were avid consumers of it, considering the art form enlightening and erotic.

Sharing *Shunga* Try leaving a book of *Shunga* images on or under the pillow for your lover to discover at bedtime. Make it an enticing erotic gift by wrapping it in black tissue paper and red silk ribbons. Enter the salacious mood by looking at the images together as you lie naked and entwined in bed.

In contrast to Western erotica, most *Shunga* lovers are depicted fully clothed (but with their robes and kimonos lifted to expose awe-inspiring genitals). Even if *Shunga* seems to be an acquired taste, allow yourself to get slowly intoxicated by a glimpse of sex in a different time. Free yourselves of inhibitions by entering into some

role play (see p26)—think of yourselves as a samurai and his bride who haven't seen each other for a long time and who wish to satiate their pent-up lust. Alternatively, study the pictures and tell your lover what turns you on about the images. Fetishize each other's genitals in true *Shunga* style—fondle or go down on each other with a feverish mixture of excitement and loving reverence.

Make your own *Shunga* Try taking some *Shunga*-style photographs of you and your lover by holding a camera in one hand as you twine your bodies around each other. Dress up in sexy underwear and capture yourselves from unusual angles. Or take a picture of your lover in a state of solo erotic abandonment as he or she lies on the bed masturbating. Take turns to be the erotic photographer. Worship each other's bodies with the camera and get wildly excited in the process.

Secret

the art of making love

Let yourselves be inspired by the artistic approach of the Japanese. Step back in time and recreate the sexually charged mood popularized in the *Shunga* drawings. Fill your bedroom with red lanterns and make slow, sensual love dressed in beautiful kimonos that slip slowly and enticingly from your bodies. Move through a series of exotic positions you've never tried before. Imagine you are posing for a series of gorgeous erotic paintings.

erotic inspiration

The Calligrapher

With yoga-like flexibility, she folds her body forward exposing her "royal gate" (vagina) and her lover presses himself inside her. She then reaches behind and clasps his legs firmly so she can remain stable as he thrusts energetically while holding on to her back for any support he might need.

FOR HER This is a dramatic position for women that ensures deliciously deep penetration, so make sure you are fully aroused and lubricated before you begin. If the sensations are overwhelming, raise your body a little and rest your hands on your knees instead. Or, for an even shallower penetration, come into a semi-standing position and lean on a wall, desk, chair, or table in front of you.

FOR BOTH If you like the naughty sense of anonymity this position brings, go one step further. Try the geisha trick of making love in complete darkness. Unleash your most sordid fantasies.

It's passionate because ... it calls for mutual trust. She's intoxicated by the submissiveness of the position and he's stimulated from playing the dominant role. If he keeps his thrusts light, fast, and shallow, she may experience an explosive orgasm. The only challenge is to remain upright.

"We were naked and he was cuddling me from behind. **I could sense he was incredibly aroused**, so I just bent over and held his legs, and allowed him to slip inside me.**"**

Twining of Swans

This position is an exciting detour to take when she has been lying on her front with him behind her. He lifts his body away from hers, giving her the space to roll onto her side. **FOR HIM** Then he sits up, lifts her leg in the air, and slips his thigh between her legs, ending up in a highly erotic scissor position in which he can thrust and she can wiggle. Ideally, he stays inside her while she tries this maneuver, but if he slips out, the couple enjoy the thrill of penetration all over again.

FOR HER He can use his hands and mouth to give his lover a thrilling array of sensations as he makes love to her. He can run his fingers up and down her raised leg, or kiss, suck, and nibble the sumptuous flesh of her thigh, and squeeze or spank her buttocks, or rake his fingers through her hair.

It's passionate because …

he has the freedom to lean over and cover her body with kisses, while he tailors his movements so the tip of his penis bumps her G-spot on each thrust. This position takes both lovers to a quivering peak of pleasure.

Take control
be his *Onna Shujin*

There is a famous Japanese legend in which a young ferryman is abducted and taken prisoner by a lady and her three maids. They keep the man imprisoned in the lady's castle and turn him into their sex slave, using him at will to service all their erotic needs.

In total command The idea of a woman taking charge—to the point where the man becomes her sex slave—can be erotic for both partners. The Japanese name given to a "mistress"—a woman who performs extreme acts of sexual dominance—is *Onna Shujin*.

If you want to be an *Onna Shujin* for the night, prepare for your role in advance. This way you can be as convincing as possible.

Power dressing Dress to look both stunning and intimidating. You will notice that the act of slipping into a particular dress can help transform your personality and put you into a commanding mindset. Try dressing as a kinky geisha. Choose a geisha dress with a fetish twist: one that skims the tops of your thighs and has a plunging neckline. Make sure the wide *obi* (sash) is drawn in tightly to emphasize the curves of your body. Alternatively, wear an open kimono over some lingerie and a pair of sexy boots or heels. Equip yourself with some kinky props, too: try a Japanese silk flogger, a dog collar, handcuffs, and blindfold. Even if you don't use all of them, the trick is to let your lover know that you might at any point.

Body language Adopt the poise of erotic power: whether your lover is lying or sitting, make sure you position yourself so that you are towering above him and asserting your dominance. Begin the evening on a thrilling note by ordering him to the bedroom. Push him onto the bed, undo your kimono, and stand over him with the ball of your foot pressed against his chest.

Throughout the evening, make sure all your movements are slow, poised, and brimming with power. When you give a command make sure your voice sounds confident and authoritative—hint at

Secret
mask yourself

This is a suggestion for women who want to ramp up their power status in true *Onna Shujin* style: make it impossible for your lover to read your expressions by wearing a traditional white *Kitsune* (fox) mask. This will immediately imply your desire to assert your animal instincts tonight. Alternatively, choose something awe-inspiringly sexy that conceals most of your face, such as a cat-eye or masquerade mask. Wear the mask, then stand in front of a mirror and be inspired to enter the role of a sex mistress. The mask should help you banish any inhibitions and unleash the sexually forceful part of you. You can be certain that this sexually dominant persona you adopt will drive your partner wild.

you belong to me **now ...**

possible "naughty" punishments if he fails to obey (and then end up administering them even if he does—it's all part of the fun).

Power games In the Japanese legend, the women delighted in keeping the ferryman in a bag with a hole cut out for his penis. They would then order him to make love to them through the bag.

Use your night of dominance to play whatever games arouse your imagination. For example, you could order your lover to massage your feet, pleasure you with a sex toy, enact a sexual fantasy, or make love to you with his hands tied (see p186). Even if he performs a task perfectly, pretend to be dissatisfied so you can exert your power. Invent some suitable punishments for being "bad." For example, make him crawl across the bedroom floor naked, or force him to wear a dog collar, or receive ten spanks or flogs. Revel in your position of dominance while allowing him to enjoy the playfulness of being under complete submission.

"When I've finally ravished you, I want you to know for certain that you gave it your all, everything you had ... that even at its fullest, your appetite was no match for mine ...**"**
* EROTIC DOUJINSHI*

New Year's Dawn

This is an ideal position for spontaneous sex because it is easy to get into. She simply braces herself against a wall and finds a firm footing with her legs apart. Neither person has to be completely undressed—he can drop his pants, then lift her skirt or dress, pull down her panties, and enter her.

FOR BOTH Try having sex with a deadline. For example, you have to finish within five minutes because you're expecting a visitor. The anxiety often increases arousal and leads to a fast, intense orgasm.

FOR HER He can get his lover in the mood by embracing her from behind and sliding his hands under her top to stroke her breasts and nipples. Touch her clitoris using gentle pressure or fleeting fingertip strokes. All the time that you are stroking her with your hands, gently kiss, lick, and nibble the sides of her neck, too.

It's ravishing because ... it fills you with an urgent sense of desire. You can do it in corridors, elevators, and even outdoors against a tree. Enjoy expending all your sexual energy and then fall dishevelled and satisfied into each other's arms.

"We were having friends over for dinner. She'd dressed up and looked gorgeous. While waiting for them to arrive, **we exchanged a knowing look** and had to have each other then and there."

Swirling River

She lies on her back and opens her legs at the widest possible angle (she may bend her legs a little). Women: if you are supple enough to do this with straight legs, invite him to watch from the side of the bed. **FOR HIM** Drive him crazy by holding your legs poised in a "V" shape as you trail your fingertips slowly up and down along the insides of your thighs. Adopt the air of a geisha skilled in slow, controlled seduction methods. Then beckon him to join you in bed.

He lies crosswise on her body and uses his chest to apply gentle pressure to her leg—this will help her to maintain her wide-open position. **FOR HER** Penetrate her slowly—this will allow her to savor the multiple erogenous sensations rippling along the sides of her vagina (the penis doesn't usually enter at this angle).

It's ravishing because ...
the intoxicating sight of her open legs gives him a strong and powerful erection. This, combined with the angle of penetration, makes her gasp, sending jolts of pleasure through her body. For a wild and unrestrained finale, slip into the missionary position.

The erotic art of tying
the *Shibari* way

Shibari is the Japanese art of bondage. Being tied up gives you the freedom to surrender completely to pleasure, as your lover teases and titillates you. Take turns to tie each other up with scarves, bondage tape, or wrist and ankle cuffs. Men, in particular, tend to enjoy this type of domination.

Tying techniques If you are a novice to the pleasures of bondage play, try this simple technique to start off the night's proceedings: First, tie your lover's hands loosely behind his back, and guide him to the bed. (This is just to give him a hint of what's to come.) Untie the knot and position your naked lover flat on his back with his arms above his head, then use bondage tape to bind his wrists and ankles together. Now that you have immobilized your lover, straddle his body on all fours and lavish him with licks, kisses, and nibbles. Treat your lover to some brief but blissful oral sex. It is important to tease your lover by alternately indulging him then pulling away—this way your lover will know that you are firmly in charge. Dominance and submission is the key to truly titillating bondage play. Afterward, swap roles so that he dominates.

Tease with your tongue If you want to take it a step further, try this Japanese tying technique: ask your naked lover to stand up and fold his arms behind his back. Now bind your lover's arms with bondage tape or a silk scarf. Tease your lover's body with your tongue in the same way as before. The fact that your lover is standing up will make him feel especially exposed and vulnerable. When your lover is quivering with arousal, guide your lover into bed, push him onto the mattress, and then let the passion take over.

For a true bondage classic, spread your lover's body in an open star shape on the bed, then tie his wrists and ankles to each of the four bedposts. You now have complete access to his body, as well as the freedom to take complete erotic advantage. Be as adventerous and daring as you want. Don't forget to swap roles.

Secret

create a naughty seat for *Shibari*

Taking sex out of the bedroom instantly ramps up the excitement factor. Add an extra frisson of naughtiness by treating a kitchen chair as a sexy *Shibari* prop: ask your lover to take a seat, then tie your lover's ankles to the bottom of the chair legs. Now ask your lover to relax their arms by their sides so you can bind the wrists to the top of each chair leg. A woman can drive her lover crazy by performing a striptease, or by lap dancing for him (see p82). A man can give his lover oral sex that takes her all the way to orgasm ... and then keep going until she begs him to stop.

sex in **shackles**

Index

Acknowledgments

Author's acknowledgments: Thanks to Suhel Ahmed for all his help, support, and ideas, and thanks to all the other members of the editorial and design team for doing such an excellent job.

The publisher would like to thank Alli Williams for hair and make-up, David Foster in his role as the photographer's assistant, Helen Murray and Charlotte Johnson for assistance at the photoshoots, Dawn Bates for editing a section of the book, Steve Crozier for helping with retouching images, Alyson Silverwood for proofreading, and Hilary Bird for the Index.